the
Bento
Book

Beauty and Simplicity in Digital Organization

Jesse Feiler

800 East 96th Street, Indianapolis, Indiana 46240 USA

the Bento Book: Beauty and Simplicity in Digital Organization

Copyright © 2009 by Pearson Education, Inc.

ISBN-13: 978-0-7897-3812-7
ISBN-10: 0-7897-3812-0

Library of Congress Cataloging-in-Publication Data:
Feiler, Jesse.
  The Bento book : beauty and simplicity in digital organization / Jesse Feiler. — 1st ed.
    p. cm.
  ISBN 978-0-7897-3812-7
  1. Database management. 2. Bento (Electronic resource) 3. Macintosh (Computer)—Programming. I. Title.
  QA76.9.D3F4378 2008
  005.74—dc22
                        2008032723

Printed in the United States of America
Second Printing: February 2009

Trademarks

Warning and Disclaimer

Bulk Sales

Que Publishing offers excellent discounts on this book when ordered in quantity for bulk purchases or special sales. For more information, please contact

U.S. Corporate and Government Sales
1-800-382-3419
corpsales@pearsontechgroup.com
For sales outside of the U.S., please contact
International Sales
international@pearson.com

Associate Publisher
Greg Wiegand

Senior Acquisitions Editor
Loretta Yates

Development Editor
Todd Brakke

Managing Editor
Kristy Hart

Project Editor
Anne Goebel

Technical Editor
Ethan Guo

Copy Editor
Chuck Hutchinson

Indexer
Erika Millen

Proofreader
San Dee Phillips

Publishing Coordinator
Cindy Teeters

Book Designer
Anne Jones

Senior Compositor
Gloria Schurick

CONTENTS AT A GLANCE

Introduction 1

1   Bento: The Database for the Rest of Us 7

2   Using the Bento Window 21

3   Working with Bento Forms 43

4   Building a Bento Library from Your Own Data 53

5   Working with Phone, URL, IM, and Address Fields and
    Lists in Contacts 65

6   Working with Bento Fields and Calculations 75

7   Expanding the Inventory Library with Related Records
    and Collections 93

8   Using Built-In Bento Libraries for Address Book 113

9   Using Built-In Bento Libraries for iCal Tasks and iCal Events 127

10 Working with Bento's Projects Library to Use Related
    Records from iCal Tasks, iCal Events, and Address Book 139

11 Designing a Projects Library with Related Notes 151

12 Building a Garden/Nature Log 165

13 Organizing a Group Project with Bento 177

14 Creating a Storyboard with Bento 189

15 Importing and Exporting Bento Data and Libraries 199

16 Managing an Email List from Constant Contact or
    Vertical Response with Bento 207

17 Bento Quickies 225

Index 233

TABLE OF CONTENTS

Introduction: Welcome to Bento…and Bento 2 1

The Database for the Rest of Us 1

How This Book Is Organized 4

    Special Features 6

Downloadable Files and Web Support 6

1 Bento: The Database for the Rest of Us 7

Introducing Bento 7

    It's All About Your Data 8

    Bento's Three Roles 8

    How Much Programming Does Bento Require? 9

    What Does "Personal" Mean? 9

Getting Started with Bento 11

Understanding Bento Terminology 13

    Fields 13

    Records 17

    Libraries 18

    Collections 18

2 Using the Bento Window 21

Getting Around the Bento Window 21

Using the Records Area 24

    Creating a New Record 27

    Entering Text Data 27

    Printing a Record 28

    Finding Data 29

    Using Advanced Find 31

    Deleting a Record 33

Using Table Views in Bento 1 33

Using Table Views in Bento 2 35

    Sorting a Table View in Bento 2 36

    Pasting Data into Table View in Bento 2 (Part 1) 36

    Editing Fields with Table View in Bento 2 36

    Pasting Data into Table View in Bento 2 (Part 2) 36

Using the Source List in Bento 1 37

Using the Fields List in Bento 1 37

Using the Libraries & Fields Pane in Bento 2 39

Setting Bento Preferences 40

3   Working with Bento Forms **43**

Working with Forms 43

Customizing a Form with Themes 47

Customizing a Form's Fields 48

4   Building a Bento Library from Your Own Data **53**

Getting Started Organizing Your Data 53

    Reviewing Your Legacy Data 54

    Working with Data Formats 54

Performing a Basic Data Import with CSV Data 57

Cleaning Up Imported Data 62

Importing Other File Formats 63

**5   Working with Phone, URL, IM, and Address Fields
    and Lists in Contacts** **65**

Exploring the Contacts Library 65

Working with Address Fields and Lists 69

    Working with Address, Email, Phone Number, and URL List
        Fields in Bento 1 69

    Working with Address, Email, Phone Number, and URL List
        Fields in Bento 2 70

Adding Address Fields and Lists to Your Forms 72

6   Working with Bento Fields and Calculations **75**

Exploring the Exercise Log 75

Creating and Formatting Date Fields in Exercise Log 77

    Creating a Stop Date Field 77

    Creating a Start Date Field 79

    Using Date and Time Field Controls 79

Creating and Formatting a Number Field in Exercise Log 81

Creating and Formatting Calculations in Exercise Log 82

    Working with the Calculation Dialog 82

    Creating the Duration Field 84

    Creating the Calories Burned Field 86

Creating and Formatting Choice Fields 87

Creating and Formatting Checkbox Fields 88

Creating and Formatting Currency Fields 89

Creating and Formatting Automatic Counter Fields 89

Creating and Formatting Rating Fields 90

Editing Bento Fields 90

**7   Expanding the Inventory Library with Related Records
and Collections** **93**

Exploring the Inventory Library 93

Creating a Library from Scratch 96

Using Relationships to Track Inventory 98

    Dragging the Related Library onto the Form 98

    Adding a Related Records List Field 100

    Formatting the Related Records List Field 101

    Summarizing a Related Records List Field 103

    Adding Data to a Related Records List Field 103

    Reviewing the Related Records 103

    Improving the Relationship and the Form 104

Using Collections 107

    Creating an Empty Collection 108

    Adding a Record to a Collection 108

    Creating a Collection from Selected Records 109

Using Smart Collections 109

8   Using Built-In Bento Libraries for Address Book **113**

Exploring the Address Book Library 113

Extending Bento's Address Book Library with New Fields and Forms 116

Synchronizing Address Book 118

Synchronizing Address Book with MobileMe 118

Synchronizing Address Book with iPhone 121

Synchronizing Address Book with PDAs and Other Devices 123

Using MobileMe Push Technology to Synchronize Data 124

Using Mac OS X Data Detectors to Update Address Book 124

9   Using Built-In Bento Libraries for iCal Tasks and iCal Events **127**

Catching Up with iCal 127

Exploring the Bento iCal Libraries 132

Using Mail's Data Detectors with iCal 134

Managing Your Calendar Data 135

Synchronizing iCal Events 137

10   Working with Bento's Projects Library to Use Related Records from iCal Tasks, iCal Events, and Address Book **139**

Exploring Projects 139

Working with Related Records from iCal and Address Book 142

Working with Related Records from Mail 146

Customizing Fields and Revising Forms 148

Add and Revise Forms 148

Creating and Sharing Calendar Events and Address Book Contacts with MobileMe 148

11   Designing a Projects Library with Related Notes **151**

Exploring the Projects Library 151

Organizing and Implementing Notes: The Basics 154

Create a New Bento Library for Notes 154

Create the Basic Field in Project Notes 156

Add a List of Related Records to the Projects Library 157

Enhancing the Relationship 161

12   Building a Garden/Nature Log **165**

Planning the Garden/Nature Log 165

Creating the Database 167

  Creating the Basic Library 167

  Creating Related Libraries 170

Analyzing the Database and Using Smart Collections 173

13   Organizing a Group Project with Bento **177**

Planning the Group Project 177

One Person = One Project 179

  Create a New Form 180

  Add a File List Field 181

  Organize Your Files 183

One Person = Many Projects 184

One Project = Many People 186

Many People = Many Projects 187

14   Creating a Storyboard with Bento **189**

Planning the Storyboard 189

  Managing Complexity with Bento 189

  Learning About Storyboards 192

Creating the Storyboard Library 192

  Implementing the Single-Value Fields 193

  Implementing the Related Record Fields 195

  Implementing Related Record Fields in iCal and Address Book 196

  Moving Forward 198

15   Importing and Exporting Bento Data and Libraries **199**

Importing and Exporting Basics 199

  Importing Data into an Existing Bento Library 200

  Exporting Bento Data 205

Importing and Exporting Libraries 206

  Exporting Bento Libraries as Templates 206

  Importing Bento Libraries as Templates 206

**16   Managing an Email List from Constant Contact or
      Vertical Response with Bento** **207**

    Learning About Email Lists and Bulk Email 207

        Communicating with Multiple People 208

        Knowing Your Way Around Bulk Email (Spam) 208

        Knowing Your Way Around Mail Filters 209

        Knowing Your Way Around ISP Rules 210

        Knowing Your Way Around the CAN-SPAM Act 210

    Using a Vendor to Send Bulk Email 211

    Moving Your Bento Email Library to and from a Vendor 213

        Uploading Bulk Email Data from Bento 213

        Downloading Bulk Email Data to Bento 220

17   Bento Quickies **225**

    Introducing Bento Quickies 225

    Nexts 226

    Software Inventory 227

    Clippings 229

    Nos 229

    Jokes 230

    Recipes 230

    Shopping Sources 231

    Fashion Parade 231

    Gift List 232

Index **233**

About the Author

Jesse Feiler has been designing databases and user-oriented solutions for two decades. He is the author of a number of books on Mac OS X, FileMaker, the Web, and a variety of other technologies such as mashups and Facebook.

A member of the FileMaker Business Alliance, he is also a developer of solutions for small businesses, nonprofit organizations (particularly those in the arts fields), publishing, and production companies. He has done many FileMaker rehabs, bringing them up to modern standards and designs. His knowledge of FileMaker and Mac OS X technologies has helped him integrate tools such as Automator into FileMaker solutions—and now into Bento.

He has worked as a developer and manager for companies such as the Federal Reserve Bank of New York (monetary policy and bank supervision), Prodigy (early Web browser), Apple (information systems), New York State Department of Health (rabies and lead poisoning), The Johnson Company (office management), and Young & Rubicam (media planning and new product development).

Active in the community, he has served on a variety of nonprofit boards including those of HB Studio and Mid-Hudson Library System, as well as zoning and planning boards. He has conducted trustee training sessions for Clinton-Essex-Franklin Library System and other groups.

Feiler's website is www.northcountryconsulting.com. The book's website is www.thebentobook.com.

Acknowledgments

Many people have contributed to this book, not least the wonderful people at FileMaker who have developed Bento. In particular, Kevin Mallon and Delfina Daves have, as always, provided wonderful assistance to the project. Ethan Guo, the product manager of Bento, helped enormously not only in discussing Bento but also in doing the technical review of the book.

At Que Publishing, Loretta Yates, senior acquisitions editor, has helped to shape the book through the editorial process. It's been a pleasure to work with Todd Brakke, Anne Goebel, Chuck Hutchinson, Erika Millen, San Dee Phillips, and Cindy Teeter, who, in various ways, have helped to make the book as clear and strong as possible.

Anne Jones, who designed the cover, managed to capture the spirit and essence of Bento in a simple design.

At Waterside Productions, Carole McClendon has, again, provided the support and assistance so important to an author.

We Want to Hear from You!

As the reader of this book, *you* are our most important critic and commentator. We value your opinion and want to know what we're doing right, what we could do better, what areas you'd like to see us publish in, and any other words of wisdom you're willing to pass our way.

As an associate publisher for Que Publishing, I welcome your comments. You can email or write me directly to let me know what you did or didn't like about this book—as well as what we can do to make our books better.

Please note that I cannot help you with technical problems related to the topic of this book. We do have a User Services group, however, where I will forward specific technical questions related to the book.

When you write, please be sure to include this book's title and author as well as your name, email address, and phone number. I will carefully review your comments and share them with the author and editors who worked on the book.

Email: feedback@quepublishing.com

Mail: Greg Wiegand
         Associate Publisher
         Que Publishing
         800 East 96th Street
         Indianapolis, IN 46240 USA

Reader Services

Visit our website and register this book at www.informit.com/title/9780789738127 for convenient access to any updates, downloads, or errata that might be available for this book.

Introduction

Welcome to
Bento…and Bento 2

IN THIS INTRODUCTIION

- The Database for the Rest of Us   1

- How This Book Is Organized   4

- Downloadable Files and Web Suport   6

The Database for the Rest of Us

Bento is a product from FileMaker, which is owned by Apple. Designed to bring FileMaker's database expertise to users of Mac OS X Leopard and later, it integrates data from iCal, Mail, and Address Book with databases that you can create from your own data as well as imported data from other sources.

Bento is lightweight in its structure but heavyweight in its capabilities. Because it builds on so many years' (actually decades') worth of experience with users and their needs both at FileMaker and at Apple, it is responsive to the frequently expressed needs and frustrations of people who need more organization than a word processing document or spreadsheet can provide but less complexity than a full-featured multiuser database might provide. Organization is the key to making information usable. Four items that are organized (ideas, recipes, addresses, bills, or shoes) can be more useful than a thousand items that are scattered around helter-skelter with no organization scheme.

Released in beta in the fall of 2007 and in a final version in early winter 2008, Bento caught on immediately. The response was positive both in reviews and in user comments. Because the Bento team is so agile and also because its design is so simple yet sophisticated, it was possible to produce a second version of the software within a year.

This book shows you how to use Bento—both the first version and Bento 2. There are significant differences to the user interface between the two versions, but the basic functionality is the same. Figure IN.1 shows one of the sample Bento libraries in Bento 1.

Figure IN.1

Bento 1 in action.

In Figure IN.2, you see the same library in Bento 2.

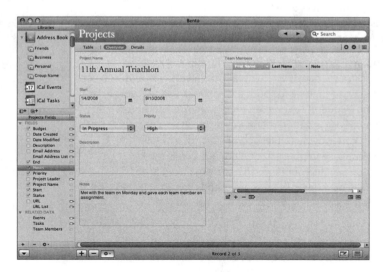

Figure IN.2

The library in Bento 2.

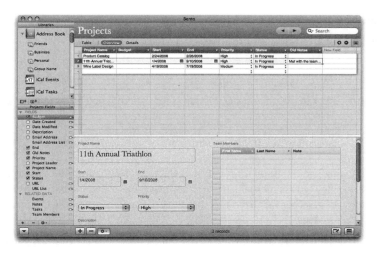 The most significant difference that you can see in comparing the two versions is that the Source list (at the left in Bento 1) and the Fields list (at the right in Bento 1) now share the same Libraries & Fields pane at the left in Bento 2. There are many other changes. One of the most important is the ability to split the main part of the window into two views, as shown in Figure IN.3. Watch for the New in This Version icon in the book for more Bento 2 features.

Figure IN.3

In Bento 2, you can split the window display in two.

There are many more changes in Bento 2. Just a few of the highlights are

- You can include messages from Apple Mail in your Bento libraries in the same way you can include iCal and Address Book data.

- You can enter data directly into the Table view, as shown at the top of Figure IN.3.

- Bento now supports more import and export formats.

- You can also save a Bento library as a template.

- Field types can be changed.

- Related records have more functionality, including the ability to click to go to a specific related record and, from that record, to return to the original record ("hot relations").

- And many, many more features as you will see in the book.

If you are still using Bento 1, have no fear. Where differences exist in functionality or the interface, both are described and illustrated.

How This Book Is Organized

This book shows you how to use Bento, and it presents a number of projects that you can use (with or without modification). The projects are designed to illustrate the types of tasks that you can perform with Bento. You may choose to mix and match features and functionality from various projects to create your own solutions.

The general structure of the book is as follows:

- In the first few chapters, you see how to use the built-in Bento libraries.
- Next, you see how to customize them.
- Then you see how to import data from another source, such as a spreadsheet.
- Finally, you see how to create and share libraries for data that you enter from scratch.

Along the way, the chapters explore various combinations of these techniques. Here is a summary of the chapters in the book:

- Chapter 1, "Bento: The Database for the Rest of Us," provides the introductory overview of Bento. It shows how you can organize your data, and it describes the basic Bento terminology, which consists of just four words. You see how to use the Bento window in both versions and how to set preferences.
- Chapter 2, "Using the Bento Window," uses the built-in Notes library to show you how to add and delete records, enter data, and find it (both using a simple and advanced find technique).
- Chapter 3, "Working with Bento Forms," uses the built-in Classes library to explore how you can customize libraries with themes, columns, labels, shading, text size, and text boxes.
- Chapter 4, "Building a Bento Library from Your Own Data," provides a quick overview of how to import data from another source such as a spreadsheet. This topic is explored in more depth in Chapter 15, "Importing and Exporting Bento Data and Libraries."
- Chapter 5, "Working with Phone, URL, IM, and Address Fields and Lists in Contacts," explores the built-in Contacts library. You see how to use multiple forms and how to work with lists of phone numbers, URLs, addresses, emails, and IMs. The integration with Mail is explored both in Bento 1 and Bento 2 (there are some differences), and you see how to add fields to a form.
- Chapter 6, "Working with Bento Fields and Calculations," shows how you can use calculation fields to make your data entry faster and more accurate. The built-in Exercise Log serves as the example.
- Chapter 7, "Expanding the Inventory Library with Related Records and Collections," delves into the concept of related records. You see how to take the built-in Inventory library and modify it so that it reflects additions or subtractions to or from inventory in a live, on-hand value.
- Chapter 8, "Using Built-In Bento Libraries for Address Book," explores one of the most powerful parts of Bento: its integration with Address Book in Mac OS X. Bento accesses the Address Book data, and it is always live in the Bento display as well as in the Address Book display. (You also see how this ties into MobileMe so that the data in Bento and Address Book is automatically synchronized with data elsewhere in your computing environment.)

- Chapter 9, "Using Built-In Bento Libraries for iCal Tasks and Events," continues to look at how Bento is automatically integrated with your data on Mac OS X. This time, the iCal data is considered.

- Chapter 10, "Working with Bento's Projects Library to Use Related Records from iCal Tasks, iCal Events, and Address Book," shows how the built-in Bento Projects library uses the technologies described in Chapters 7 through 9. Related records from the built-in Mac OS X applications are associated with specific projects. This allows integration so that, for example, iCal can display tasks and events over a period of time and across many projects while you can view each project separately in Bento. Furthermore, the integration of iCal and Address Book with MobileMe means that your Bento tasks, events, and contacts are automatically available on all your synchronized devices from Macs to PCs to iPhones. This chapter also shows the new Bento 2 feature that lets you integrate messages from Mail with your Bento libraries.

- Chapter 11, "Designing a Projects Library with Related Notes," shows how you can customize the built-in Projects library with structured notes. This capability allows you to enter and browse comment and note data by date or other categories. Notes differ from tasks and events not only in that they are stored totally in Bento, not in iCal, but also because notes are a record of what has happened and been discussed in a project—the past, as well as the future events and tasks. For many people, this library may be all the project tracking they need.

- Chapter 12, "Building a Garden/Nature Log," builds a customized project from scratch. This project is good for a kid, class, or family. It integrates observations, measurements, and photos of a garden or natural world with Bento. It also shows how you can perform complex or tricky calculations with Bento's summary row and Smart Collections (as in calculating the last frost date—a date that is characterized by the fact that you do not know the date of the last frost until all possible subsequent frosts have not happened).

- Chapter 13, "Organizing a Group Project with Bento," shows how to use Bento as the core of a multiuser project. Bento is designed for a single user, but this is a great way for a person (teacher? project leader? committee chair?) to pull a group project together.

- Chapter 14, "Creating a Storyboard with Bento," focuses on organizing a visual project and shows how you can keep track of all the related storyboard project aspects, such as locations, costumes, actors, and props. You can also integrate notes and visuals into the storyboard itself. Storyboard can help you organize everything from a political commercial to a family history.

- Chapter 15, "Importing and Exporting Bento Data and Libraries," explores Bento data import and export. You also see how to use the Bento 2 features that allow you to create and use your own Bento library templates.

- Chapter 16, "Managing an Email List from Constant Contact or Vertical Response with Bento," takes a common real-word problem and explores how you can use Bento to help you. Managing an email list is more than just tracking names and addresses. In this chapter you see the basics of importing and exporting addresses to and from the major bulk-mailing programs.

- Chapter 17, "Bento Quickies," provides tips and suggestions for a number of projects. Because you have already seen how to use Bento, these quickies can point you in interesting directions in just a paragraph or two.

Special Features

This book includes the following special features:

- **Chapter roadmaps:** At the beginning of each chapter is a list of the top-level topics addressed in that chapter. This list enables you to quickly see the information the chapter contains.

- **Notes:** Notes provide additional commentary or explanation that doesn't fit neatly into the surrounding text. Notes give detailed explanations of how something works, alternative ways of performing a task, and other tidbits to get you on your way.

- **Tips:** This element gives you shortcuts, workarounds, and ways to avoid pitfalls.

- **Cautions:** Every once in a while there is something that can have serious repercussions if done incorrectly (or, rarely, if done at all). Cautions give you a heads-up.

- **New** **New in This Version icon:** This icon identifies new features in Bento 2.

- ↩ **Cross-references:** Many topics are connected to other topics in various ways. Cross-references help you link related information together, no matter where that information appears in the book. When another section is related to one you are reading, a cross-reference directs you to a specific page in the book on which you can find the related information.

Downloadable Files and Web Support

For updates to the book, see the author's website, www.northcountryconsulting.com and the book's website, www.thebentobook.com. There is also a Facebook Page for the book at www.facebook.com/pages/The-Bento-Book/23722243212.

Downloadable files for this book are available on the Web:

- www.thebentobook.com.

- www.informit.com/title/9780789738127

FileMaker is the developer of Bento. There are a number of resources on the FileMaker site:

- www.filemaker.com/bento gets you to the basic Bento page.

- There is a discussion forum for Bento at http://forums.filemaker.com/fmbnto/.

Bento: The Database for the Rest of Us

IN THIS CHAPTER

- Introducing Bento   7
- Getting Started with Bento   11
- Understanding Bento Terminology   13

Introducing Bento

Built on Mac OS X 10.5 ("Leopard"), Bento is a personal database from FileMaker. A wholly owned subsidiary of Apple, FileMaker has sold more than 13 million units of easy-to-use database software, which runs on both Windows and Mac OS X for individuals; companies large and small; as well as education, government, and research organizations. FileMaker's long experience in the database world, and the company's key understanding of how users use—and don't use—databases is how Bento is made possible. At the same time, Bento is made possible not just by Apple's Max OS X operating system, but also by Apple's decades of experience in how people use—and want to use—computers and other devices such as the iPod and iPhone.

When you first launch Bento, you will find yourself in an environment you already know. Because Bento uses the same specific interface elements that you know from applications such as iPhoto, iCal, and iTunes, what you see when it opens is just your basic Mac OS X application interface. Why should you have to work differently if you are dealing with photos or with music or with appointments? If you want to move a chair from one side of the room to another, you do it the same way in which you move a plant from one windowsill to another. (But you are still going to need help with that sofa.)

It's All About Your Data

What is it about your computer—your *personal* computer—that you value most? If it is from Apple, the sophisticated design of the hardware and intuitive look-and-feel of the interface may come to mind first. You may have applications on your computer that you simply could not live without: for some people, life is unthinkable without Adobe Photoshop or InDesign; for others, it is Quicken or Microsoft Excel; and for many Mac users, the components of iLife (iPhoto, iTunes, iWeb, iDVD, and Garage Band) or those of iWork (Numbers, Keynote, and Pages) are the indispensables.

But it is your data—and not these applications—that is generally most valuable to you: the list of your friends and colleagues inside your contacts file; the bills and payments in your accounting software; the music in your music library; the papers you have written for school; and the contracts you have prepared for your business. These are the items that you protect with frequent backups using technologies such as Time Machine, MobileMe, and iSync as well as external backups to CDs or tapes as needed.

Apple has been a leader in making information accessible. Address Book and Apple Mail share data easily; tools such as Services, AppleScript, and Automator make it easy to create complex tasks such as moving data from a FileMaker database to an InDesign document and then on to a printer without your needing to do anything more than click a mouse.

Until Bento came along, there was one important area that was unfinished. It is very hard for people to come to grips with the fact that while a powerful yet simple application such as Address Book lets you easily store names, addresses, job titles, nicknames, birthdays, and even pictures, there is no simple way to store a friend's favorite song in an Address Book record—even though the song may be in your iTunes library. This isn't a specific problem with Address Book or iTunes; it is a problem that has existed for decades in the computer world. By and large, the application designer has to make it possible for information to be stored and shared. Adding a data element that the designer has prepared for (a birthday) is a no-brainer. Adding a data element that has not been prepared for (a favorite song) can be a monumental task.

Not only is it difficult to add new data elements to existing applications, it is also often extremely difficult to get information out of the walled fortresses that many applications seem to be. (Although Services, AppleScript, and Automator are an enormous help, not every application supports them.) That is why many people have a list of names and addresses in Address Book, another such list in an accounting program, yet another in a project management database, and so on.

Bento's Three Roles

Bento provides three related roles to help you address your data needs. First, it lets you store data— any data in a database of your own. Regardless of whether it is a household inventory, guests at a party, or minutes of a meeting, you can store it in Bento.

But Bento goes beyond that. It gives you access to data from Address Book and iCal that is already on your computer. This is not a copy of the data: it is the Address Book and iCal data itself. Make a change in Address Book to someone's phone number, and you see the changed number immediately in Bento. There is only one place where the data is stored, but Bento can see it and update it.

Similarly, Bento can access media and other files on your computer. As with Address Book and iCal data, this data remains where it is, but Bento can display it.

New In Bento 2, email messages, notes, and RSS articles in the built-in Mac OS X Mail application join the list of data on your computer that Bento can access. Just as with Address Book and iCal data along with files, the data remains where it is, but it is visible to Bento, and you can work with it through Bento. In the case of Mail, you can drag the messages that matter to a specific Bento record into a message list. You can then view a message in Quick Look, or you can open one or more messages in Mail with the click of a button.

And finally, Bento solves the favorite-song issue. You can view Address Book data in Bento, selecting the editable fields that you want displayed. You set the format and layout of the data. And if you want that favorite song, you can add it to your Bento data display from Address Book. When you are looking at Bento, you do not see that some of the data comes from Address Book and other data (the favorite song, for example) comes from somewhere else. It is all together in Bento: just as you want it to be.

If you want to organize your data your way, Bento is for you. Bento is not about figuring out where your data is or how it is stored. It's about what data you want to see and how you want to see it. "Seeing" in this sense means more than just viewing it: you can change it in Bento and it is changed wherever it is stored, whether that is inside Bento itself or in iCal, Address Book, or Mail.

So that is what Bento is: a personal database for your data, organized and displayed just the way you want it, without your worrying about anything else.

How Much Programming Does Bento Require?

There is a one-word answer to the question of how much programming Bento requires: none. Programming generally requires you to describe the processes that you want to have happen. (It is frequently called *procedural programming*.) Although the terminology is different, it is similar to writing out a set of instructions for a recipe or for changing a tire. Do this, then do that, and then…. The sequence ("then") is important.

In Bento and some other modern databases, you don't worry about the recipe: you just create the structure of your data from a real-world point of view—not a programmer's point of view. An entry in your Address Book can have a name and an address; it also (in your Bento version) can have a favorite song for that person. There is no sequential process for manipulating the data. For example, in Bento, you could find all your friends whose favorite song is *Summertime*. Or you could go the other way and find the favorite songs of all your friends who live in Denver.

All Bento asks is that you think about how the data is related to itself, and that is a simple process.

What Does "Personal" Mean?

Beyond the obvious meaning, the word "personal" has some important implications in the world of Bento and personal databases. Most important, your Bento personal database is tied not just to yourself, but also to your computer (or, more specifically, to a given account if you are sharing a computer with other people). Large-scale databases can usually be networked either locally or over the Internet. Bento is not designed to be networked. Each Bento database is designed to work for a single user on a single computer.

TIP

You can use some of the tools for sharing Bento libraries that are described in Chapter 15, "Importing and Exporting Bento Data and Libraries," to use Bento on several computers.

The single Bento environment exists for a given user on a given computer. If you share a computer, your account has its own Bento database, and other accounts on that computer (perhaps for other members of your family) have their own Bento databases. If you do not share your computer, you still have an account, but it may not be obvious to you. Go to System Preferences and select Accounts. You see the window shown in Figure 1.1.

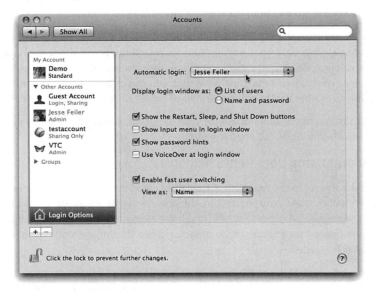

Figure 1.1

Create accounts and manage automatic login from System Preferences.

Login Options at the lower left of the window brings up the options shown at the right. If Automatic Login is enabled, it is set at the top of those options. (To change the options, you need to unlock the window by clicking on the padlock icon and supplying an administrator password.) In the default Mac OS X installation, a single user account is created, and it is set to automatically be logged in, so you may not realize that you have your own account, but you do.

You can also use this window to create other accounts on your computer. If you are sharing the computer, it is possible that you have been doing so just by organizing folders for each member of the household. It is preferable to go to System Preferences and create separate accounts for each user. In that way, each user is able to set his or her preferences for various features using System Preferences. Because Bento stores a user's database in a specific location inside that user's account, only one Bento database can exist for each user. (That is why using folders within a single account works for documents that you can move around, but it does not work for Bento.)

TIP

If you have separate folders for various users within your own account, you can easily create accounts for them as described previously, and you can let them copy their files from folders in your account to their new accounts. Simply move those folders (properly named, of course) to your Public folder. Then, when a new user logs in, they can find your Public folder if they go to the hard disk and then select the Users folder, the name of your account, and then the Public folder. From there, the user can drag the appropriate folder into his or her own Documents (or other) folder.

Getting Started with Bento

Bento may come pre-installed on your computer. If not, you can download it from the URLs listed in the Introduction. You can also order a shrink-wrapped package with a CD from www.filemaker.com.

TIP

Because Bento can access data from Address Book and iCal (as well as from Mail in Bento 2), it will help you if you have some data in Address Book and iCal as well as Mail. If you have not used Address Book or iCal, you may want to enter a little data in them: two addresses will do for Address Book; and two each of iCal Tasks (To Dos) and iCal Events (specific dates and times).

When you first launch Bento, you see the Home dialog, as shown in Figure 1.2. You can watch a movie about Bento, set up Bento for Address Book or iCal, and get started either by creating a new library or dismissing the dialog with Start Using Bento.

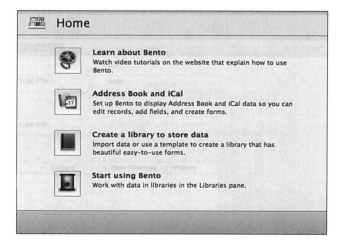

Figure 1.2

Use the Home dialog the first time you launch Bento.

You can always reopen this dialog with Window > Home. Use Bento > Preferences to open the Preferences dialog shown in Figure 1.3. In the When Bento Starts section of the dialog, you can control whether the Home dialog is shown each time you launch Bento.

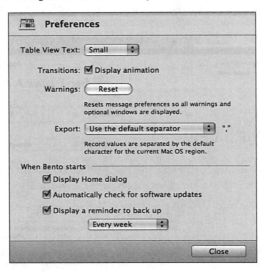

Figure 1.3

Use Preferences to control whether Bento 1 displays the Home dialog at startup.

In Bento 2, a variety of export formats are available in the Preferences dialog, as shown in Figure 1.4. These are discussed further in Chapter 15.

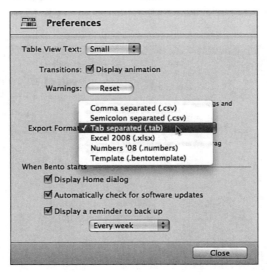

Figure 1.4

Bento 2 preferences include new file export formats.

You can set up Bento for Address Book or iCal from the Home dialog, but you can also do it at any time from File > Address Book and iCal Setup.

> **NOTE**
>
> In this chapter, you will find the basics of Bento. Later in the book, you will find step-by-step walk-throughs describing how to create your own Bento libraries. In this overview, the focus is on what to do and how to talk about Bento and the interface elements in the Bento window. The screenshots are taken from various Bento templates that you will find installed for you in Bento. The different screenshots are designed to give you an idea not only of what you can do with Bento, but also what it can look like. In later chapters, you will see how to create your own libraries and customize the Bento templates.

Understanding Bento Terminology

Like all databases, Bento lets you manage data. Data can be of all types: text, numbers, graphics, videos, and music; in addition, Bento lets you treat files, folders, and email messages on your Mac as data. Databases help you organize data, and, in doing so, you need to structure that data. In Bento, the data structuring is simple. It relies on fields, records, libraries, and collections. All of them exist within your Bento environment. Although you can have many libraries (containing records with fields in them), you have only a single Bento environment that includes all your libraries and other Bento entities.

> **NOTE**
>
> Your Bento environment is located inside your Home folder in Library/Application Support/Bento. Do not move or rename this folder. Launch Bento, and it automatically opens the appropriate file. In general, stay out of the Library folder unless you are absolutely certain of what you are doing.

In the sections that follow, you will find the specific details of fields and records: these are concepts that are common to modern databases. Two other concepts—libraries and collections—are specific to Bento.

Fields

A field contains a single data element such as a phone number or a picture. In Bento, it can be a file or folder, and that object itself can contain more data. In Bento 2, references to email messages in Mail can be stored in fields.

> This section provides an overview of Bento's fields. For more information about creating fields and working with the Fields dialog, see Chapter 6, "Working with Bento Fields and Calculations," p. 77.

Each field in Bento has a name and a *type*, such as text, number, or checkbox. A person's weight is a number; that person's name is text. Bento defines several field types that are common to many databases. Several of the fields have options that you can set, such as the number of decimal places and whether to use a thousands separator in a number field. To define fields and set their options, you use the Fields dialog, shown in Figure 1.5 and described more fully in Chapter 6. The names of fields must be unique in the library. (Libraries are described later in this section.)

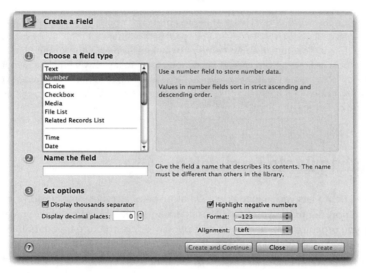

Figure 1.5

Create fields and set their options in the Fields dialog.

Starting in Bento 2, you can change the type of a field after you create it. Bento converts existing data to the new type. In Bento 1, after you create a field, you cannot change its type. Because not all field types can be converted to all other field types, Bento shows you only the types to which a given field can be converted.

Bento's formatting of fields is based on the settings you provide in System Preferences in Mac OS X. In the International pane, you can select the language you prefer to use as well as the formats to be used. In Figure 1.6 you can see different settings for English/U.S. and French/Switzerland.

NOTE

In the Fields dialog (refer to Figure 1.5), you have a checkbox option to set whether you use the thousands separator in displaying a number. What that thousands separator (a comma, dot, or space) separates is determined in the Formats tab of the International pane of System Preferences.

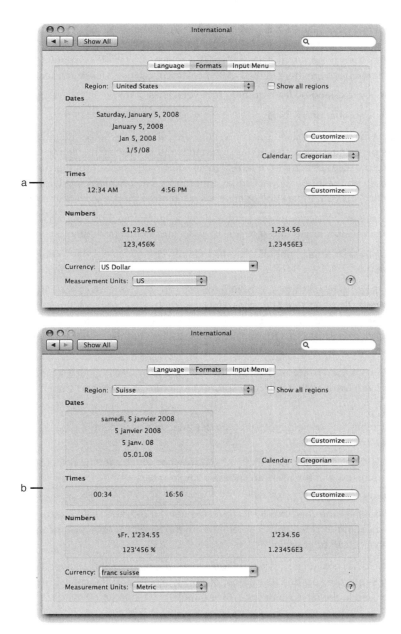

Figure 1.6

International formatting preferences for English/U.S. (a) and French/Switzerland (b).

It is important to note that Mac OS X is presenting data in various ways regardless of how the under-lying data is formatted. Applications generally store dates, numbers, and currency values in format-neutral ways. They then present that data to Mac OS X, which applies the current International format options. Bento continues from there in the field types described in the following section:

- *Text* is for any text ranging from nothing to several lines of text.

- *Number* is a number of any kind.

- *Currency* is for currency values. You can set the currency type, whether negative numbers are shown in parentheses or with a minus sign, and whether they are highlighted. You can also determine the alignment (right or left) of the value. Finally, you can set the currency symbol. This is based on the International Format preferences, but you can refine it for specific fields in Bento, which lets you display one or more values in other than your default currency.

- *Time* contains an hour and minute value. When you create the field, you can indicate that it is displayed as a Short format (no seconds) or a Medium format (including seconds).

- A *duration* field stores a period of time; the field can contain weeks, days, hours, minutes, and seconds either as full words or as their one-letter abbreviations (w, d, h, m, s).

- *Date* is a date. There are three sets of options you can set. The first lets you display Month and Year or Month, Day, and Year. The second lets you choose the format—Short (9/25/2008), Medium (Sep 25, 2008), Long (September 25, 2008), or Full (day, September 25, 2008). Finally, you can click a checkbox to add the time to the display—either in Short or Medium format as described previously in the time field.

- A *media* field is used to store a picture, movie, or sound (music). If your Mac includes a camera, Bento lets you use it so that you can capture the picture or movie and store it directly in Bento.

In addition, Bento has several field types that are designed not only to store data, but also to present it in special ways on the interface:

- A *choice* field has a list of values that you specify when you create the field. They are presented as a popup menu, and the user can choose a single value.

- A *checkbox* field has a name, and it is presented with that name and a checkbox. The user can select or deselect the checkbox indicating whether the checkbox value is true or false. Note that this meaning of "checkbox" is different from the basic Mac interface meaning where more than one value can be checked.

- A *rating* field has a value from 1 to 10. (You can set the range that is allowed.) When it is displayed in Bento, the appropriate number of stars is shown, and you can highlight how many are to be used in the rating (3 out of 5, for example).

- An *automatic counter* is an automatically generated number for each record that is created. It is unique for each record in a library; you can specify its starting value and the amount by which it is to be incremented. Normally, both of those values are 1. You will see how to use a counter in Chapter 6.

Next, there are three list field types that let you present multiple items in a single scrolling list field.

- A *file list* field contains aliases to files. Double-clicking an item in the file list field opens that file using the default application for that file or file type.

- A *related records list* field contains records that you have selected from another Bento library. In Bento 2, you can click a button to go to a selected related record; from there you can click another button to return to the initial record.

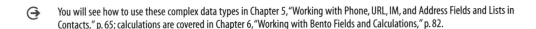 There is more information on related records in Chapter 7, "Expanding the Inventory Library with Related Records and Collections," p. 98.

- In Bento 2, a *message list* field contains email messages, RSS articles, and notes from Mail.

As is the case with many databases, you can create *calculation* field types: they store the result of a calculation that often involves the data from other fields. If you have a field called temp_farenheit that contains the temperature in Farenheit, you can create a calculation field called temp_celsius that calculates the appropriate value. Calculations can also include values such as today's date that are not stored in fields. Furthermore, calculations can produce results that are themselves a text value or a number, date, time, duration, or currency. For example, if you have separate fields for first and last names, you can create a calculation field to combine them and to insert a space between them.

Lastly, there are five complex data types you can use. These combine several fields in a single data structure. For example, the address data type provides space for several addresses along with a label (home, work, other, or a custom label) for each one.

- Address
- Phone Number
- Email Address
- URL
- IM Address

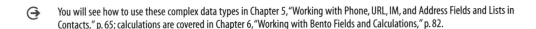 You will see how to use these complex data types in Chapter 5, "Working with Phone, URL, IM, and Address Fields and Lists in Contacts," p. 65; calculations are covered in Chapter 6, "Working with Bento Fields and Calculations," p. 82.

Records

Bento data is stored in fields, and the fields are stored in *records*. Each record within a Bento library contains the same fields although the values are different. A record often corresponds to a real-life entity: a student, an inventory item, or a motion at a meeting. The record's fields could be name and class for a student, price and size for an inventory item, or wording and result of a vote for a resolution.

When you think about your Bento data, you can envision it as a table or spreadsheet with the columns representing fields and the rows representing records. If your data does not fit into that type of tabular structure, you may need to rethink it. For example, if you want to keep track of all your data—your bank accounts, your favorite songs, your photos, your friends, important dates to remember for your family, and your family tree—you can see that set of data does not lend itself to the row/column structure. But there is a solution. Because Bento lets you relate data to other data in your Bento database, you can split up your data into substructures that are two dimensional: a list of bank accounts, list of songs, list of photos, and so forth. Each of these sets of records and their fields makes a neat two-dimensional table, and you can combine them in Bento into a composite view of your data.

When it comes to database design, "divide and conquer" is often a good strategy. Furthermore, putting too much together into a too complex data structure is often a dead-end route. Start small and use Bento to help join your component parts together.

➔   Bringing data together involves creating *relationships*. You will find more about this topic in Chapter 7, "Expanding the Inventory Library with Related Records and Calculations," p. 98.

Libraries

A *library* is a set of records in Bento. As noted previously, you have a single Bento environment, but you can have many libraries within it. When you launch Bento for the first time, normally you have several libraries that are already created from your Address Book and iCal. You can create other libraries from Bento templates or build them yourself from scratch.

➔   For more on Bento's interface to Address Book, see Chapter 8, "Using Built-In Bento Libraries for Address Book," p. 113. For the iCal interface, see Chapter 9, "Using Built-In Bento Libraries for iCal Tasks and iCal Events," p. 127.

Although from a data point of view, libraries contain records, they also contain interface elements such as forms that are described in Chapter 2, "Using the Bento Window."

Collections

The structure described so far is simple: fields contain data elements, and they are organized into records. Your libraries consist of records that you can add and delete as you add or delete data.

You can also create *collections*. These are collections of records within a library that you create using Bento. They are comparable to playlists in iTunes, albums in iPhoto, or groups in Address Book. They could be attendees at a meeting or inventory items that a specific customer purchases. Collections appear in the Source list underneath the library to which they belong. They are slightly indented, and their icons are a bit smaller than the library icon.

In Figure 1.7, you can see two collections that are part of the Inventory library (Sale Items and Smart Sale). Groups from Address Book (Friends, Business, and Personal) are shown in Bento as collections. As you will see later in this section, collections can be assembled manually, or they can be Smart Collections that are automatically created based on criteria that you set. The small triangle to the left of the library's icon lets you expand or contract the library so that its collections are or are not shown.

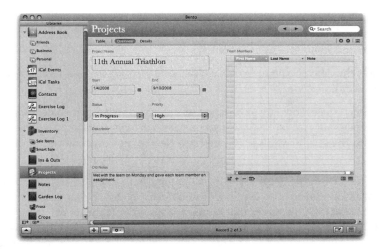

Figure 1.7

You can organize a library's records into collections.

Collections introduce one of the key elements of digital organization: digital objects can be in more than one place at a time. In the physical world, a document is in one drawer of a file cabinet or another drawer. If you take it out and put it on your desk, it is no longer in the file cabinet. You can make a copy of the document and put the copy on your desk, but you now have two versions of the document. If you make a note on the copy of the document that is on your desk, that note is on that copy, and it is not on the original version of the document in the file cabinet.

In the digital world, this basic rule of physics does not apply. You can have a record that is located in a library in Bento. That much is like the physical world, and, in fact, the record can be in only one library.

But if you create a collection, you can add that record to the collection, and that has no effect on the original record. When you view the record through the collection, you are looking at the record in its own Bento library: you are not looking at a copy. If you change the record data while viewing it in a collection, that change immediately is reflected in the record that is part of the Bento library (because it is the same record).

You can add a given record to many collections. There are no limits to the number of collections in which a record can reside. No matter how many collections it is in, there is only one version of the record; any change that you make to it in any collection or in the original Bento library is reflected everywhere the record is shown. If you delete the record from the Bento library, it is deleted everywhere.

However, if you delete a record from a collection, you delete it only from that collection: it still exists in every other collection to which it was added, and, of course, it still exists in the Bento library where it started out.

Powerful as collections are, *Smart Collections* are even more powerful. These are collections that are automatically updated. You create them by setting up criteria based on data values in a record's fields.

Any record that matches those criteria is automatically added to the Smart Collection. Smart Collections are directly comparable to Smart Folders in the Finder, Smart Playlists in iTunes, Smart Albums in iPhoto, and Smart Groups in Address Book.

In Figure 1.7, note the difference in the icons: under the Projects library, Sale Items is a collection, and Smart Sale is a Smart Collection.

You can create Smart Collections in two ways, just as is the case with Smart Folders and the other smart objects throughout Mac OS X. The first way is to search for certain data and save that search as a Smart Collection. The second way is to choose File > New Smart Collection and specify the search to be used.

Thereafter, whenever a record is created that matches the criteria in the Smart Collection, it shows up in the Smart Collection. If the basic record from the library is deleted, it disappears from the Smart Collection. And, if a data value changes, that causes a record to no longer match the criteria; it disappears from the Smart Collection but remains in the library. By the same token, if a data value changes in a library record in such a way that the record is now valid for a Smart Collection, it appears in the Smart Collection.

As with collections, you can have as many Smart Collections as you want, and as many records as you want can be in as many collections and Smart Collections.

TIP

As you experiment with Smart Collections, you will find some of the power of Bento. After the Smart Collection is set up, records come and go automatically. As you continue working with Bento, you can think about Smart Collections as you are laying out your fields and records. By creating fields that lend themselves to being criteria for Smart Collections, you can make your Bento database more dynamic.

For more details on collections and Smart Collections, see Chapter 7, "Expanding the Inventory Library with Related Records and Collections," p. 107.

2

Using the Bento Window

Getting Around the Bento Window

Like iTunes and iPhoto, Bento has a single window that you work in. (By comparison, applications such as Keynote, Numbers, and Pages let you have multiple windows open at a time.) Figure 2.1 shows the Bento 1 window.

IN THIS CHAPTER

■ Getting Around the Bento Window   21

■ Using the Records Area   24

■ Using Table Views in Bento 1   33

■ Using Table Views in Bento 2   35

■ Using the Source List in Bento 1   37

■ Using the Fields List in Bento 1   37

■ Using the Libraries & Fields Pane in Bento 2   39

■ Setting Bento Preferences   40

Figure 2.1

Use the Bento window to manage your Bento data (Bento 1).

The window in this figure shows the Projects library, which is one of the templates included with Bento. It is not only a template in Bento, but also an actual library with a multitude of data records so that you can explore Bento and its navigation.

In addition to the window frame, there are three main sections of the window: the *Records area* in the center, the *Fields list* at the right, and the *Source list* at the left. (Window sections like these are called *panes* in the Mac OS X interface.) In the bottom frame, a control lets you choose what panes to display. As you can see in Figure 2.2, the options in this control let you have any combination of panes provided that the Records area is visible.

Figure 2.2

Control what sections of the Bento window are displayed (Bento 1).

The library that you select from the Source list is the library that is shown in the Records area. If the Fields list is visible, it contains the fields for that library.

 In Bento 2, the Bento window has the same three sections, but they are rearranged as you can see in Figure 2.3.

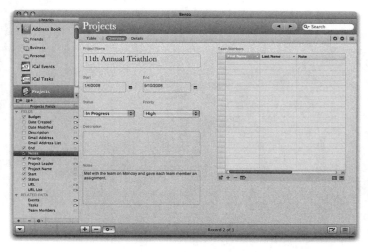

Figure 2.3

In Bento 2, the main window layout has changed.

Instead of the Source list at the list at the left and the Fields list at the right, a single Libraries & Fields pane at the left combines the information. Libraries are shown in a scrolling list at the top; at the bottom, the fields for the selected project are displayed. You can drag the divider between these two lists so that one is larger than the other—or not visible. The Libraries pane is always visible, but the triangle in the lower-left corner of the window shows and hides the Fields pane. Thus, if you have enlarged the Libraries pane to take up the entire Libraries & Fields pane at the left of the window, that button makes the Fields pane visible and you can resize it as you want.

To create a new library, either choose File > New Library or use the Add a Library button (+) from the bottom of the Source list (Bento 1) or the Libraries pane (Bento 2). Either action lets you choose from Bento's templates for libraries, as shown in Figure 2.4.

Figure 2.4

Use the New Library dialog to create a library.

The templates are organized into groups. Some templates appear in more than one. For more information, select the library template you are interested in with a single click. Information about it appears at the bottom of the New Library dialog.

The Import Data button in the lower-left corner of the New Library dialog lets you import data. You can also use File > Import to import data.

For more information on importing data, see Chapter 4, "Building a Bento Library from Your Own Data," p. 54 and Chapter 15, "Importing and Exporting Bento Data and Libraries," p. 199.

In Bento 2, the File > Import command lets you choose between a file and a template. If you choose to import a template, you can create your own library based on a template you or someone else has created. There is more on this in Chapter 15, "Importing and Exporting Bento Data and Libraries."

The name of the library starts out as the name of the template, but the Name field is editable so that you can change it before you create it. When you have chosen the library you want, click Choose in the lower-right corner of the dialog to create it. Alternatively, double-click the library template to create it.

You can then look more closely at the library. If you realize that it is not quite what you are looking for, you can either modify it or try again. To delete a library, select it in the Source list and choose Edit > Delete Library. You can also select it and delete it with the Delete key at the upper right of the keyboard.

For now, create a Notes library from the template, as shown in Figure 2.5. This library is selected because its data structure is as simple as possible. There are no collections and no related records, so it is a good place to start with Bento basics.

NOTE

Table views, the Source and Fields lists (Bento 1), and the Fields & Records pane (Bento 2) are discussed separately in this chapter because there are significant differences in their interface elements in the two versions.

Using the Records Area

Having created a new library from a template, you will notice that a single record is present. You can use it as an example for further entries, you can modify its data, or you can delete it. For now, leave it as is.

In Bento 2, see the control shown previously in Figure 2.2 to show only the Records area. (You can also use View > Show > Records Only.) In Bento 2, choose View > Hide Libraries & Fields Pane to get the same result.

Bento works within the size of its window, which you can resize in the normal way from the lower-right corner. If you choose to show only the Records area, the window retains its size, and the display of the Records area grows to fill the window. Figure 2.5 shows the Records area after you have created a new Notes library from the template.

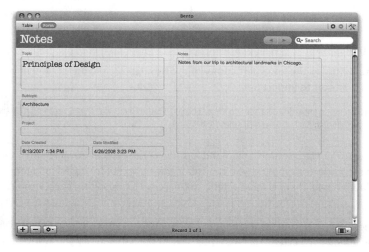

Figure 2.5

Create a new library from the Notes template.

In the *navigation bar* at the top of the window, you can choose to view the data in a table view; if you do so, you see the table shown in Figure 2.6. (The navigation bar also contains the library name, next and previous arrows, and the search field; these are discussed later in this chapter in the "Finding Data" section.)

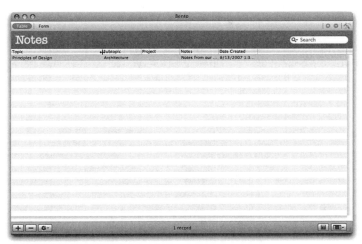

Figure 2.6
Use the table view in Bento 1.

As you can see in Figure 2.6, you can resize columns in the table view.

New Figure 2.7 shows the Bento 2 table view.

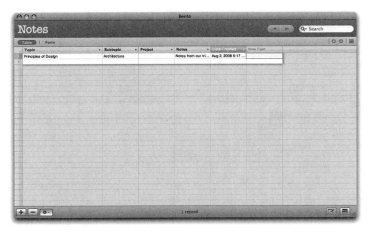

Figure 2.7
Use the table view in Bento 2.

At the top of the Records area, you can select a form that lets you view a single record, rather than the list of records shown in a table view. For the Notes library, this form is called Form, which is the default name for a new form.

↪   You see how to create new forms and rename them in Chapter 3, "Working with Bento Forms," p. 46.

 In Bento 2, you can also show the Records area in a split view, with a table view at the top and a form view at the bottom, as shown in Figure 2.8. As you can see in Figure 2.8, you can move the divider between table view at the top and form view at the bottom so that you see more or less table or form.

Figure 2.8

Use the split view to see a table and form view together.

You control the split view with View > Split View or the button that shows or hides the split view at the upper right of the Records area, as shown in Figure 2.9.

Figure 2.9

Show or hide the split view.

Creating a New Record

In form or table view, create a new record in any of these ways:

- Choose Records > New Record to create a blank record.
- Choose Records > Duplicate Record to duplicate a record; you can then modify the data. Use this technique if you need a record that is similar to an existing one.
- Use the Add a Record button (+) at the bottom of the Records area.

 In Bento 2, there is always a blank line at the bottom of the table view. You can just start to type your data there without using an explicit command. As soon as you click or tab out of the first field in which you have entered data, a new record with that data is created, and a new blank line below it appears in the table view.

When you create a new record in any of these ways, you see a nearly blank record. In the default Notes library, the Date Created field is filled in with the current date and time. This field is present in every Bento record (along with Date Modified). You can use these fields to search for records created or modified at certain times. You do not have to display the fields, but they can be useful for trouble-shooting.

By default, you are in the first field, which in this case is Topic. You can tab from field to field: the order in a form is from top to bottom in the first column and then top to bottom in the second column. You cannot change the order, but you can move the fields so that they are entered in a logical sequence.

➔ For more information on changing the look of a form, see Chapter 3, "Working with Bento Forms," p. 47. For more information on changing the look of a table view, see the sections "Using Table Views in Bento 1 and 2" later in this chapter.

Entering Text Data

Enter text data by typing or by using the Clipboard to copy and paste it from elsewhere in Bento or anywhere else on your computer. Bento takes care of the formatting automatically. You can do this either in form or table views.

There are a few special commands you can use to assist you in entering text data. To enter the current date and time, choose Insert > Current Date and Time. You can use this command in a date or time field as well as in a text field, and you can modify the value (for example, to change today's date to a properly formatted date for tomorrow just by changing the day number).

When it comes to text data, you can use the built-in Mac OS X spelling features that are available in the Edit > Spelling submenu. You can check spelling at any time; you can also choose to check spelling as you type. Either way, misspelled words are underlined with dots, as shown in Figure 2.10.

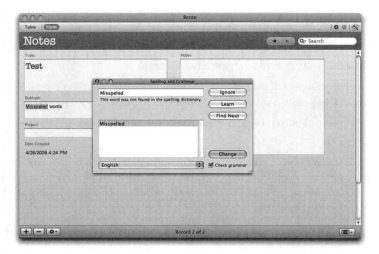

Figure 2.10
Check spelling and grammar.

Also in the Edit > Spelling submenu is the Show/Hide Grammar and Spelling command, which is what shows or hides the window shown at the front in Figure 2.10. This feature lets you correct a word (although you can do that simply by changing the highlighted word), but you can also add it to your dictionary. Just like Bento, your dictionary is specific to your Mac OS X user account; if you add a word to your dictionary, it is added for any Mac OS X applications that use the built-in spelling feature.

TIP

Add words you use frequently to your dictionary and turn on Check Spelling While Typing for the best results. By adding your own commonly used words to your dictionary, you avoid warning of misspelled words that are actually correctly spelled but not in the default diction-ary. By automatically flagging possible spelling errors (and minimizing false positives), you get in the habit of correcting words quickly.

As the book moves through different types of libraries in its examples, you will find details of entering data for other types of fields.

Printing a Record

Whether for a hard-copy backup or to share information with other people, you often need to print out Bento data. Choosing File > Print or Print from the Additional commands button at the bottom of the Records area does the trick. Either one brings up the dialog shown in Figure 2.11.

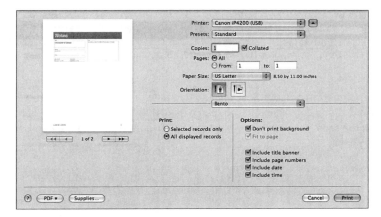

Figure 2.11

Print Bento data.

One thing you will notice immediately is that this dialog includes the orientation and page size settings that you are used to finding in a Page Setup command. The preview at the left of the dialog is live, so you can see how your settings affect the printed version of the data.

The most important setting is the radio buttons toward the center of the dialog that let you control whether all displayed records are to be printed or only the selected records. If you have searched for records, those are the selected records; if you are browsing a record, it is the only selected record. You can manually create a set of selected records in a table view by selecting more than one record; as always, Shift-click the first and last records in a contiguous list and Command-click the various records in a noncontiguous list.

You can use this setting together with the page printing settings to determine what the total set of printable records is (with the radio buttons) and then which of those are to be printed.

The checkboxes at the right of the dialog let you control the formatting of the printout. One of the most important settings here is whether to print the background. Some elegant color combinations that work on the screen do not work well on printed copies—particularly if they are to be printed on a black-and-white printer or photocopied or faxed. In those cases, you might not want to print the background.

Finding Data

Before continuing with this chapter, enter at least two more records into the Notes library using the techniques described previously in this chapter. The reason for entering the data is so that you can experiment with finding and sorting data as described next.

It does not matter what data you enter or what fields you use. In the Notes library, you can enter unique names in the Topic field. ("Test" and "Another Test" are fine to use.) The limitation of unique names is only for experimenting with finding data. Bento has no problem handling multiple records with identical field values and keeping them properly separate.

⊖   In Chapter 4, "Building a Bento Library from Your Own Data," p. 57, you see how to import data into Bento. When you have mastered those techniques, you can use sample libraries and data from the book's website as described in the Introduction. (There are some constraints in Bento 1; Bento 2 allows the direct import of Bento libraries.)

Whether you are using form or table view, you can find data in your library. The simplest way of doing so is to type a word, phrase, or value into the search field at the upper right of the Bento window. Bento carries out the search as you type in the search field and shows you the number of records found, as you can see in Figure 2.12.

Figure 2.12

Search for data.

Bento handles data conversion for you automatically. In Figure 2.12, for example, the search is for the word "test." Two records are found: Test and Another Test if you have entered the data suggested previously. The display of the number of records found disappears after a few seconds, but the bottom of the Bento window shows you how many records have been found. You can switch back and forth between form and table views; the records you have found remain. To see all records, delete the search criterion either by clicking the small round X or by deleting the text. (This is the same searching interface you find in Spotlight and other Mac OS X searches.)

NOTE

Summaries in table view reflect the records that have been found, not the entire set of records.

If you experiment with your test data, you will see that you can find whole words, parts of words, and even single characters within a word. You do not need to specify wildcards or special symbols to do this: it just happens.

Figure 2.12 shows another Bento feature that is available in form view. Arrows let you move to the next and previous record; they are located to the left of the search field. In most cases, using Find is faster than manually searching through the library with next and previous arrows unless you are dealing with structured data that is inherently sequenced (such as appointments by date or time) and that has been sorted.

Using Advanced Find

You can use Advanced Find to create more sophisticated searches. You can go to Advanced Find either by choosing Records > Advanced Find or by clicking the small downward arrow next to the magnifying glass at the left of the search field. As you can see from Figure 2.13, that downward arrow brings up a contextual menu that lets you go to Advanced Search, repeat recent searches, or clear the search history.

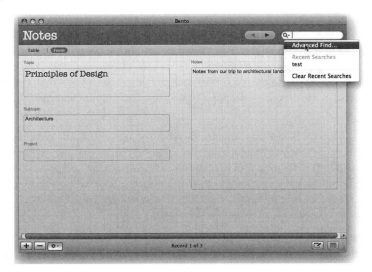

Figure 2.13
Find more search options.

Figure 2.14 shows the Advanced Find features. You may very well have seen them before in Spotlight, the Finder, and other applications. (Note that Figure 2.14 shows the Advanced Find as you might set it up and before you click the Find button.)

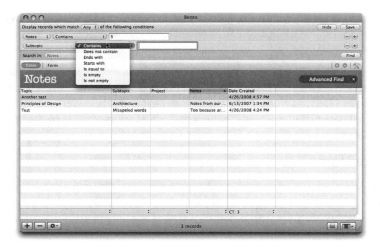

Figure 2.14

Use Advanced Find.

Starting from the top of the window shown in Figure 2.14, there are three sections of Advanced Find. They provide a compact and powerful interface to Bento's searching capabilities. You can set up several search criteria if you want; you also can make each of them more specific than the simple find mechanism described in the preceding section. (That is how, for example, you can find Another Test but not Test.)

In the first row at the top of the window, you decide whether you want all the conditions to be applied or any of them. *All* (a logical *and* in database parlance) means that they all have to be true. *Any* (a logical *or*) means that if even one is true, the record is selected. In complex databases, more combinations can be set up: you can combine a set of conditions, all of which must be true with a second set in which any can be true, and you can further specify other types of logical operators. For Bento, however, these two logical operators are sufficient.

Next, you specify the conditions. Each condition is applied to a field, and, as shown in Figure 2.14, you can specify what the logical test is. Finally, you specify the value to be tested. To add more conditions, click the + at the right of the row; to remove a condition, click –.

Finally, you click Find at the bottom right of the Advanced Find section. The search is then carried out. At the top right, you can see that you can hide the Advanced Find section. This capability is useful if you need to check some data values in the Records pane. Particularly if your Advanced Find has a number of criteria, you may not be able to see as much data as you want. Hiding Advanced Find does not destroy your search criteria. When you show Advanced Find again, everything is still there.

→   At the upper right of the Advanced Find area, you can save your search. In fact, you create a Smart Collection that is based on the search. As you add (or delete) records in your library, the Advanced Find is applied to each record and the Smart Collection always shows the results of the Advanced Find. This process is described in detail in Chapter 7, "Expanding the Inventory Library with Related Records and Collections," p. 109.

Because of the speed of Bento's finds, and because you can build such complex Advanced Find searches, it is a good idea to use those tools rather than repeatedly sorting and manually searching the data. There are several tips that can help you use Bento's find mechanism quickly and productively. Here are a few of them:

- Use the simplest search possible to start.

- Although sorting the entire library is often unnecessary, combine sorting with searches. If you have several hundred (or thousand) names in your Address Book, you can quickly search on a company name and last name to find the person you are looking for. But if you can't quite remember the name, try searching on the company name first and then sorting the results by last name. As long as the find is active (that is, until you clear it with the X at the right of the find search field), only the found records are displayed or sorted.

- Think about how you will be searching for data as you build your library. Many manufacturers and distributors identify their products with a stock-keeping unit (SKU) code. If you will be using a SKU, place it in its own field so that you can easily look it up. If you enter it as part of the name of the product, you may wind up accidentally retrieving the wrong data elements because sometimes a SKU is already part of a title as in "Handle for briefcase SKU1." The actual handle SKU might be SKU2.

Deleting a Record

To delete a record, select it in table view or display it in form view and choose Records > Delete Selected Record(s) or use the – button at the lower left of the Records area. (In table view, you can select several records for deletion at once.)

TIP

Make certain you really want to delete the data. When it is gone, it is gone forever, except for copies that you may have in Time Machine or your Bento backups. If you are cleaning up a Bento library and deleting a lot of data, it is an excellent idea to use the backup and exporting features described in Chapter 15, "Importing and Exporting Bento Data and Libraries," before you delete data.

In addition, you can use a Smart Collection as described in Chapter 7, "Expanding the Inventory Library with Related Records and Collections," to create the appearance of deleting data without actually deleting it.

Using Table Views in Bento 1

Table views let you see more than one record at a time from the library you are using. This allows you to do a number of things that you cannot do in form view when you are looking at one record at a time:

- You can sort records based on the values in any column.

- You can summarize the data in one or more columns.

You can resize columns by dragging the dividers in the title row. You can also change the order of the columns by dragging the titles left or right until the order is what you want.

Figure 2.15 shows three records in the Notes library's table view. They are used in this section.

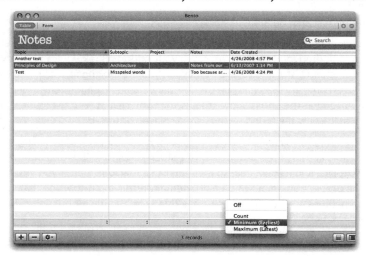

Figure 2.15

Sort and summarize columns in table view.

First, note that the Topic column is highlighted, and a small indicator at the right of the column title shows that it is sorted. To sort a column, click on its title. It indicates how it has been sorted; to change the sort order (from low-to-high to high-to-low, for example), just click again.

SORTING IN BENTO

One column at a time can be highlighted and sorted, but previous sorts remain in place. Thus, you can do a two-level sort. For example, you can sort a First Name column and then sort a Last Name column to give you a table that is sorted by Last Name and First Name. You sort the columns in reverse order with the secondary sort such as First Name being the first one you perform. This procedure is simple, intuitive, and fast in Bento.

In addition, sorting is often unnecessary. Many database experts believe that sorting databases is the most unnecessary thing that people do with their databases. And, although Bento sorting is fast, sorting a large database can require significant computer resources to complete. Most people sort a database to keep it organized so that they can quickly look at it and see notes, names, or the like in alphabetical order. In most cases, this is unnecessary. Although the database may look organized to you, alphabetizing data so that you can quickly find what you are looking for is much more time-intensive than simply searching for the data you want. As you have seen, Bento has powerful search tools available, and there is generally no need for you to manually search an alphabetized list.

Although sorting is often unnecessary, summarizing data is frequently helpful. In table view, you can have a summary row at the bottom of the table, as shown in Figure 2.15. You control its visibility by choosing View > Show/Hide Summary Row, or you can use the button at the lower right of the Records area of the Bento window (just to the left of the control that lets you choose which panes are shown).

Depending on its type, each column has its own summary options. At the very least, each column can be counted. This is a count of the number of values in that column, not the number of records in the table view. For numeric fields, you can summarize using a sum, average, minimum, or maximum in addition to the count. As shown in Figure 2.15, a date or time field can be summarized by minimum/earliest or maximum/latest in addition to count. If the summary row is visible, these summary values are automatically updated in table view as necessary.

To keep an up-to-date count of the number of records in a library, use the count summary function and apply it to the Date Created field. Because Bento always fills this field as soon as a record is created, counting the number of values gives you the number of records.

Using Table Views in Bento 2

Table views let you see more than one record at a time from the library you are using. This allows you to do a number of things that you cannot do in form view when you are looking at one record at a time. In Bento 1, there were two of these features:

- You can sort records based on the values in any column.
- You can summarize the data in one or more columns.

New In Bento 2, you can paste data into multiple records and fields in table view. In addition, the small triangle at the top of each column in Bento 2 lets you edit the table structure using a contextual menu, as shown in Figure 2.16.

Figure 2.16

Use the contextual menu from the triangle at the top of each column data in table view to sort and edit the table and its data in Bento 2.

You can resize columns by dragging the dividers in the title row. You can also change the order of the columns by dragging the titles left or right until the order is what you want.

The same three records shown previously in Figure 2.15 for Bento 1 are used in this section. In Bento 2, the triangle does not show the direction of the sort. You control-click it to bring up the contextual menu shown in Figure 2.16.

Sorting a Table View in Bento 2

Although only one column at a time can be highlighted and sorted, previous sorts remain in place. Thus, you can do a two-level sort. For example, you can sort a First Name column and then sort a Last Name column to give you a table that is sorted by Last Name and First Name. You sort the columns in reverse order with the secondary sort such as First Name being the first one you perform. This procedure is simple, intuitive, and fast in Bento.

Pasting Data into Table View in Bento 2 (Part 1)

New In table views in Bento 2, there is always a blank row at the bottom of the records displayed. As soon as you type in the first field (whatever field it is), a new record in the library is created. If you are pasting a column of data from a spreadsheet into Bento 2, it creates as many records as are necessary to store the values in the spreadsheet column.

TIP

This behavior applies to tabular data copied from spreadsheets as well as from tables in word processing applications such as Pages and Microsoft Word. A table that is constructed from tabs, spaces, and other formatting symbols is not a table in this sense. A table is one that is constructed in Microsoft Word by using Table > Insert Table > Table or Table > Convert > Text to Table. In Pages, it is a table constructed with Insert > Table. Many other applications provide similar functionality.

Editing Fields with Table View in Bento 2

As you can see from the contextual menu shown in Figure 2.16, in addition to sorting a selected column, you can add or delete fields before or after the selected column, hide or duplicate the field shown in the column, edit the field name, or change its type. These commands are also available in the Libraries & Fields pane; they are discussed in the "Using the Libraries & Fields Pane in Bento 2" section later in this chapter.

For now, what is important to note is that in table view in Bento 2, in addition to being able to create a new record in the blank row that is always visible, you can add fields in the table view. An extra column is always available at the right in the same way that an extra row is always visible at the bottom. After you tab out of this new field, a new column is created, and a new extra column appears to the right of the added column. (Added fields are visible in the table view as well as all forms view if you choose to use them.)

Pasting Data into Table View in Bento 2 (Part 2)

If you select more than one column in a table or spreadsheet, you can paste the data into a table view in Bento 2. In the previous section, it was noted that if more rows are needed, they are automatically created. If your Bento list view needs more columns for the data, they, too, are created.

This means that in an extreme case, you can create a Bento 2 library with one record and one field. You can then select an entire spreadsheet or table from Microsoft Word or Pages and paste it into that one field in the one record. Bento adds as many records and fields as it needs to accommodate all the data. You can then use the contextual menus to change field types and names.

Using the Source List in Bento 1

If it is shown at all, the Source list is at the left of the Records area, as shown in Figure 2.17.

As you create a new library, it is added to the end of the Source list. You can rearrange libraries by dragging them up and down. As you see in Chapter 7, you can create collections and Smart Collections that are based on libraries. They are shown beneath the library on which they are based; you can use the small disclosure triangle next to a library's icon to show or hide its collections.

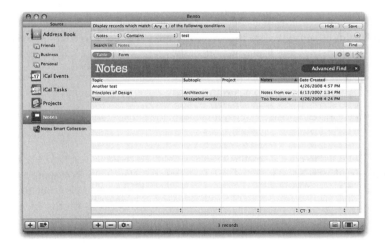

Figure 2.17
The Source list shows libraries and collections in Bento 1.

In Figure 2.17, the Address Book library has three collections. (These groups were set up in Address Book.) Beneath the Notes library, you can see a Smart Collection icon. In this case, it contains the Advanced Search shown at the right of Figure 2.17. You can name a collection or Smart Collection anything you want.

Using the Fields List in Bento 1

You can choose whether you want to show the Fields list; if it is shown, it appears at the right of the Records area, as shown in Figure 2.18.

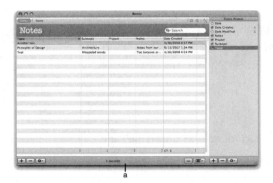

Figure 2.18

Use the Fields list in Bento 1 in table view (a) and form view (b).

In table view (see Figure 2.18.a), a small checkbox to the left of each field name indicates if it is shown in table view. (All fields in table view are shown as columns.) You can drag columns in table view to change the way in which they are displayed, and, as shown previously, you can resize them.

In form view (see Figure 2.18.b), a small box is located next to each field. To add a field to a form, simply drag it to the form. If there is no arrow in a box, it has already been added to the form.

⊖   For more information on creating forms, see Chapter 3, "Working with Bento Forms," page 46.

You can use the Fields list to create, delete, or rename fields. To create a new field, use the Add a Field button at the lower left of the Fields list (+) or choose Insert > New Field. To rename a field, double-click it to open the Edit the Text Field dialog, as shown in Figure 2.19. To delete a field, select it and choose Edit > Delete Field or click the Delete the selected fields button (–) at the lower left of the Fields list.

There is a Duplicate Field command in the Edit menu; it is also available in the Additional Commands list at the bottom of the Fields list. If you want to create several similar fields with the same formatting or other features, just duplicate the original field and change the name using the dialog shown in Figure 2.19.

Some fields have a padlock to their right. These fields are controlled by Bento; they cannot be deleted or renamed.

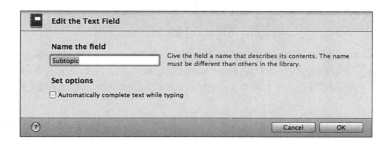

Figure 2.19

Edit a field.

Using the Libraries & Fields Pane in Bento 2

The former Source and Fields lists are combined into a Libraries & Fields pane in Bento 2. If it is shown at all, the Libraries list is at the top of the Libraries & Fields pane at the left of the Bento window, as shown in Figure 2.20. If the Libraries & Fields pane is not shown, choose View > Show Libraries & Fields pane.

Figure 2.20

The Libraries list in the Libraries & Fields pane shows the libraries in Bento 2.

As you create a new library, it is added to the end of the list. You can rearrange libraries by dragging them up and down. As you see in Chapter 7, you can create collections and Smart Collections that are based on libraries. They are shown beneath the library on which they are based; you can use the small disclosure triangle next to a library's icon to show or hide its collections.

In Figure 2.20, the Address Book library has three collections. (These groups were set up in Address Book.) Beneath the Notes library, you can see a Smart Collection icon. In this case, the Advanced Search shown at the right of Figure 2.20 has been saved as Test Projects, which is the Smart Collection.

In the lower part of the Libraries & Fields pane, similar functionality to the Fields list at the right of the Bento 1 window is provided. The most basic difference is that the checkboxes that control whether a field is shown in the table view are at the left of each field name. The indicators to the right of each field name let you see whether you can add that field to the selected form.

You also will see related records in a different way than you did in the Bento 1 Fields list. You can add a field by clicking the + button at the bottom of the list; to delete a field, select it and choose –. In the other actions icon, you will find commands to edit the field as in Bento 1 and to change its type, a new feature in Bento 2.

 For more information on working with fields, see Chapter 6, "Working with Bento Fields and Calculations," page 77.

Setting Bento Preferences

To set Bento's preferences, you choose Bento > Preferences to open the dialog shown in Figure 2.21.

These preferences affect Bento's behavior and appearance across all libraries. If you want to change the behavior or appearance of individual libraries, Chapter 3, "Working with Bento Forms," provides that information.

The chief difference between Bento 1 and Bento 2 is that in Bento 1, you can choose what delimiter to use for exporting data in CSV format: commas, semicolons, or the localized default. In Bento 2, you have a wider variety of export choices. Remember that this is your default setting; you can override it for individual exports.

Also useful is the Reset button. It restores Bento to its defaults so that warnings and optional windows are always displayed.

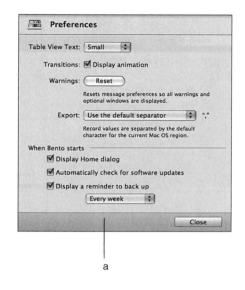

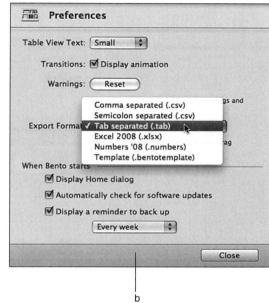

Figure 2.21

Set preferences in Bento 1 (a) and Bento 2 (b).

3

Working with Bento Forms

IN THIS CHAPTER

- Working with Forms 43
- Customizing a Form with Themes 47
- Customizing a Form's Fields 48

Working with Forms

In Chapter 2, "Using the Bento Window," you saw how to use the Fields list (Bento 1) or Libraries & Fields pane (Bento 2) to add fields. This chapter continues the discussion of fields and forms.

Every Bento library can be shown in a table view. At the top of the Bento window, you will see that for that library you can select either the table view or a form view. The table view is identified as "Table"; you can name the form views—and, yes, there can be more than one form view for a Bento library, but there can only be one table view.

This chapter begins by exploring the Classes template; its table view is shown in Figure 3.1. It contains a single record that is part of the template.

Figure 3.1

Display the Classes template in table view in Bento 1.

The table view in Bento 2 is much the same as you can see in Figure 3.2. The biggest difference is that in Bento 1, the table view looks like iTunes, whereas in Bento 2, it looks more like a spreadsheet.

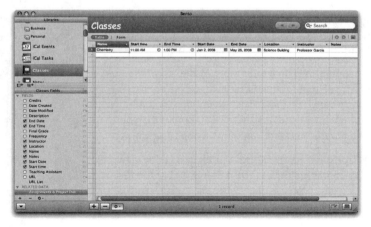

Figure 3.2

Display the Classes template in table view in Bento 2.

The differences in functionality were described in Chapter 2. As far as the fields in the library that are shown in the table view, the difference is that the list is at the lower left in Bento 2 and at the right in Bento 1. In both cases, you select the fields to be shown in the table view by using the checkbox to the left of the field name. Because there is only one table view in a library, whether a field is displayed in that table view is an attribute of the field, and it can be set in the Fields list.

You can switch from table view to form view by clicking Form at the upper left of the Records area. The Classes form view is shown in Figure 3.3 as it appears in Bento 1.

Figure 3.3

You can view the data in form view in Bento 1.

There are more differences between Bento 1 and Bento 2 when it comes to form views. Compare Figure 3.4, the Bento 2 version of the form, with Figure 3.3, the Bento 1 version.

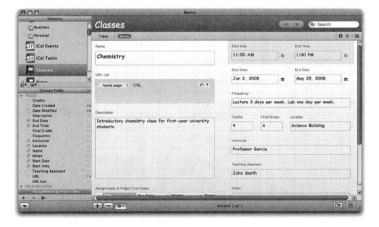

Figure 3.4

The Classes form view is shown in Bento 2.

First, note that in Bento 1, to the left of each field name is a small icon that indicates if that field can be dragged into the form. (The field is not already in the form because a field can only appear in a form once.) That icon appears in Bento 2 to the right of each field name. As you switch from one form to another, the icons are updated in both Bento 1 and Bento 2 to reflect whether you can add the field to the form.

Note that in Bento 2, the Fields list makes a distinction between fields in the current library and those in related data. You can see this clearly in the Assignments & Projects field, a field that shows related records from iCal. In Bento 2, it clearly shows up as a related records field, whereas in Bento 1, it and any other related records fields are displayed alongside the library's fields.

In form view, you are able to rename a form, create new forms, and delete a form. (Except for the last one; there must always be at least one form in the library.)

To change a form's name, double-click its name to open the dialog shown in Figure 3.5. (This is the name of the form itself; it appears to the right of Table and among any other forms. To change the name of the library, click its name—Classes in this case.) You can also use Forms > Rename Form. Here, the form in the template is called Form. For this chapter, you are modifying that form. The safest way to do that is to rename it "Original Form" and then to duplicate it and work on the duplicate. Thus, Figure 3.5 shows you the first step in the process.

Figure 3.5

Rename a form.

The second step is to duplicate the form by choosing Insert > Duplicate Form in Bento 1 or Forms > Duplicate Form in Bento 2. Bento then duplicates the original form; its default name has "Copy" at the end. The next step is to rename the duplicate form from "Original Form Copy" to "My Form." Now you are ready to go.

Customizing a Form with Themes

Like Keynote with its styles, Bento lets you apply visual themes to your forms. These coordinated appearances combine a selection of colors and fonts in various styles. With a form selected, you can change its theme by choosing Format > Theme. Unlike Keynote, Bento does not allow you to change the details of the themes. However, because of the large number of provided themes, you are likely to find themes that you like.

A Bento theme is totally separate from your data. That means you can switch themes at any time without affecting your data. The various templates use a variety of themes, but you can change them at will.

If you want to be sophisticated about your Bento themes, you can select several of them to use for specific purposes, such as displaying confidential data from work, displaying social data, and the like.

Themes are applied to the active form; when you next go to a table view, that theme is applied to the table. If you then go to a form in the library that uses a different theme, that other theme is applied to the table view when you navigate from the second form to the table view.

With Bento 2, there are more than two dozen themes available. You can select a theme from Forms > Choose Theme. The first item in the submenu is Theme Chooser. It lets you select a theme and try it out. The Bento window behind the Theme Chooser dialog is visible using the new theme.

Some examples of Bento themes are shown in Figure 3.6.

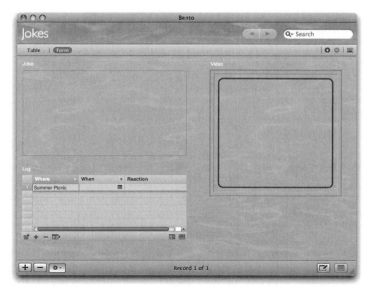

Figure 3.6

Bento has a variety of themes.

Customizing a Form's Fields

To customize a library's table view, you use the Fields list (to control which fields are shown) and directly manipulate the table. You can reorder columns, show or hide the summary row, and change column width. In Bento 1, you modify a form view by choosing View > Customize Form or by clicking the customize form button at the upper right of the Records area. In either case, the search field is replaced by Customize Form with an X to its right. To exit from Customize Form, click that X.

New In Bento 2, you can customize a form by clicking on the edge of a field to move or change it. Figure 3.7 shows how you can access the customization options for a form. If you click in the field itself, you are able to enter data. Clicking on its border shows handles that you can use to resize the field, as shown in Figure 3.7. When the handles are visible, you can drag on the field's border to move it. If you click in the center of the field, the handles disappear, and you are able to enter data. This and the other interface elements described in this section replace the Customize Form mode in Bento 1.

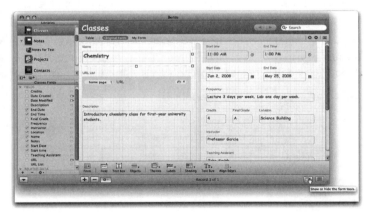

Figure 3.7
Move and reshape fields in Bento 2.

When you start to customize a form in Bento 1, new tools appear at the bottom of the form view; in addition, guides appear on the form. Among the customization tools is a Themes tool that lets you select themes just as you can do by choosing Format > Themes. In Bento 2, a button in the lower-right corner of the window controls whether the form tools are shown or hidden as does View > Show Form Tools, as shown in Figure 3.7.

Bento puts the labels in the appropriate location and coordinates their appearance with the appearance of the relevant field using the currently selected theme. When you drag a field from the Fields list or Libraries & Fields pane into a form that you are editing, an outline of the label and data field appears as soon as you move your mouse into the Records area, as shown in Figure 3.8.

Figure 3.8

Bento automatically provides the label and data entry fields.

Some fields require more than one data entry element; if so, they are shown in the outline and are placed in the form as soon as you release the mouse button. A heavy line shows you where in the form the new field and label are placed. In Figure 3.8, a URL list is being placed on the form; it is one of the field types that require several elements for display and entry.

For more details about these composite data fields, see Chapter 5, "Working with Phone, URL, IM, and Address Fields and Lists in Contacts," p. 69.

After a field and its label have been placed on a form, you can change its width or height by selecting it and dragging the right or bottom border. You can also rearrange fields; just drag them up or down or from column to column. Everything is taken care of for you by Bento: fields move aside as needed. And, of course, the tab order remains logical (top to bottom and left to right in column one, and then on to column two with the same ordering). To rearrange fields after you have already added them, in Bento 1 you choose View > Customize Form, and in Bento 2, you click the border of a field to begin editing it.

Bento provides you with several formatting objects that you can add to a form. Figure 3.9 illustrates three of them.

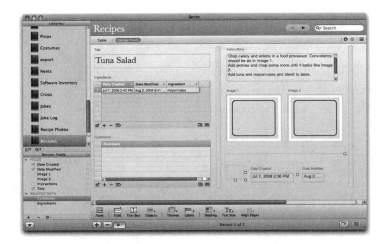

Figure 3.9

Use form objects to help format a form.

The line beneath the two images is a *horizontal separator*. Another object, a *spacer*, has been added before the Date Created field. Also, a column separator has been added to the right of the column containing the images. Of these objects, only the horizontal separator is visible when you have finished editing the form (by clicking in another field or going to another form). Figure 3.10 shows the result. You can tell that a third column has been added to the form by the position of the horizontal scrollbar at the bottom of the form. In Figure 3.10, it has been moved so that the third column is visible.

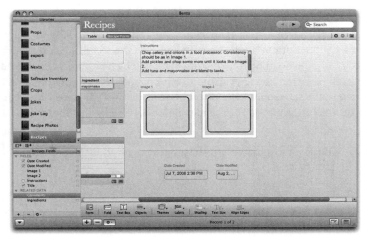

Figure 3.10

Only the horizontal rule is directly visible in the finished form.

The Form tools in Bento 1 and Bento 2 are mostly the same, but there are some differences. Table 3.1 describes each of the tools from left to right and provides keyboard equivalents. In the case of tools that are different in the two versions, that difference is noted. If no version difference is indicated, the tool works the same in both Bento 1 and Bento 2.

NOTE

Figures illustrating the use of the various tools are referenced in Table 3.1. Some of them occur in later chapters.

Table 3.1   Form Tools

Tool	Equivalent	Purpose	Version Differences
Form	Double-click form name in the navigation bar or Forms > Rename Form.	Change a form's name (Figure 3.5).	Bento 2
Field	Opens the Create a Field dialog	Open the Create a Field dialog (Figure 6.2).	Bento 2 In Bento 1, a choice in the Objects tool
Text Box	Insert > Text Box	You can type anything you want in the text box, and you can move it around the form just like a field. Unlike a field, this is not data from your library; it is simply text that appears on the form.	Bento 2 In Bento 1, a choice in the Objects tool
Objects	Insert > Horizontal Separator Insert > Column Divider Insert > Spacer	A spacer is a blank area that also can be moved around. You use it to add space between fields. There is also a horizontal separator (a line) that can be used to separate groups of fields.	See Field, Text Box, and Columns for Bento 1 differences
Related Data	Insert > Related Records List	Open the Create a Field dialog with Related Records List selected for Field Type.	Bento 1
Themes	Bento 1: Format > Theme Bento 2: Forms > Choose Theme	Select a theme.	Theme Chooser only available as the first choice in Bento 2

Continues...

Table 3.1   Form Tools (continued)

Tool	Equivalent	Purpose	Version Differences
Columns	Format > Columns	Choose 1-5 columns for the form.	Bento 1
Labels	Bento 1: Format > Labels Bento 2: Forms > Labels	Choose Above or Beside for position of labels on all fields in the form.	Bento 2: can also choose small, medium, and large size
Shading	Bento 1: Format > Shading Bento 2: Forms > Shading	Choose None, Light, or Dark for selected field(s).	
Text Size	Bento 1: Format > Text Size Bento 2: Forms > Text Size	Choose Smallest to Largest for selected field(s).	
Align Edges	Bento 2: Forms > Align Right Edges	Align right edges of selected objects. Other edges remain where they were.	

TIP

Be wary of going overboard with these design elements. If you find yourself needing to organize your forms with spacers and separators, maybe you would be better off splitting your form into two separate forms. As you see in Chapter 7, "Expanding the Inventory Library with Related Records and Collections," you can use collections and related records to bring whole sets of data onto a form in a simple way. Bento works best for most people when you can see all the data elements in a form without scrolling the window.

The field consists of the label and the data entry section(s); a background may be shaded for the entire rectangle that contains these elements. In the Format menu or the tools at the bottom of the Customize Form view, you can choose the degree of shading you want. They can be effective in highlighting essential (or nonessential) information as long as you use shading consistently.

You can also change the size of the text in the data fields, although the size of the label text is changeable only in Bento 2. Finally, you can select two or more fields and align their right edges. You do this by expanding the narrower fields' widths so that all are consistent.

4

Building a Bento Library from Your Own Data

IN THIS CHAPTER

- Getting Started Organizing Your Data   53

- Performing a Basic Data Import with CSV Data   57

- Cleaning Up Imported Data   62

- Importing Other File Formats   63

Getting Started Organizing Your Data

In the first few chapters of this book, you saw the basics of Bento: how to use the Bento window, how to create and delete records, and how to use the Bento data management tools such as finding and sorting. You even saw how to create databases from the Bento templates and started finding out how you can customize the look and feel of your personal databases.

This chapter helps you move in a new direction. You know the Bento basics; now what can you actually—practically—use it for in your own life? The acid test is whether Bento can help you organize all the data you have floating around your computer. Many people have accumulated lots of data over the years. Computer disks have grown bigger and bigger; if you buy a new computer periodically, the hard disk will be larger than the one you are used to, and you might be able to move all your data from the old crowded computer and its hard disk to the new hard disk and have plenty of space left over.

The data can consist of old email and documents that just might be needed some day; it can be in the form of spreadsheets and even a variety of database formats large and small. Maybe you have AppleWorks files that you rely on for your daily activities. The format may be old, but the data is valuable and—most important—you can get to it.

This chapter shows you how to go about moving data into Bento, where it can be stored and searched quickly. If you are using old software to manage your data, you may legitimately be worried that at some point or another the software may break and you may not be able to find a new version, leaving your data inaccessible. (The term for such data and software is *legacy*, as in legacy software or legacy data.) Although you probably do not want to think about it, the fact is that data stored in old software and unsupported formats is a critical risk to any person or organization that relies on it.

⮕   Importing data into a new library as described in this chapter is simpler than importing data into an existing library. For more details on importing and exporting data and libraries including new file types supported in Bento 2, see Chapter 15, "Importing and Exporting Bento Data and Libraries," p. 199.

Reviewing Your Legacy Data

Moving data into Bento is not difficult, and it is something that you should do for your legacy data. But pace yourself. First, if you haven't already, protect your most important data and the data for which your applications are old and not easily replaced or updated. Often, the easiest way to do this is to move them into Bento.

Data that you move into Bento is going to wind up as a set of records with fields in them because that is the basic Bento paradigm. Often, you move data from spreadsheets or database tables because those are comparable structures. Sometimes, the data is in word processing documents formatted as a table. Free-format data that is not tabular in nature is not a particularly good candidate for Bento import.

NOTE

Importing is used to describe the process of reading a file and converting it into one or more Bento records automatically. Even the most free-format data can still be moved into Bento by copying and pasting each data element individually into a Bento record. It is the automated process that works best with tabular data.

Working with Data Formats

You can import references to files in Bento, so your movies, free-form poetry, and other data are accessible and organized by Bento. However, remember that the application that Bento uses to open the file needs to be available. Storing a reference to a file that needs to be opened by a program you do not have or that is no longer available does not do you any good.

Fortunately, many programs allow you to save your documents in alternate formats. These are generally available in Save As or Export commands located in the File menu. Figure 4.1 shows the Microsoft Word Save As menu.

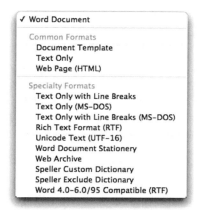

Figure 4.1

Many applications let you save a copy of a file in a new format.

These formats are a combination of proprietary formats and formats that are widely available. Many programs support older versions of their native formats for reading and writing. Word, for example, lets you save backward-compatible files going back to Word 4.0. You can also save the basic text in a variety of formats; these files can be opened by any program that can read text. Rich Text Format (RTF) is a standard format that preserves a great deal of style information including fonts and basic paragraph formatting. Saving old word processing files in RTF or a text-based format makes them accessible by many programs.

The iWork applications Pages and Numbers use an Export command, as shown in Figure 4.2.

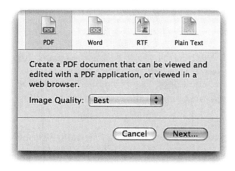
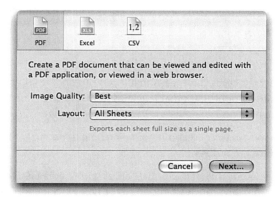

Figure 4.2

iWork applications use the Export command.

Notice that you can save Numbers files as native Excel spreadsheets and you can save Pages files as native Word documents. Plain text and RTF are also supported in Pages, while comma-separated value (CSV) is supported in Numbers. Both support Portable Document Format (PDF).

A standard installation of Mac OS X includes TextEdit, which can read and write both plain text and RTF files. This means that if you convert old files to either of those formats, you are able to store references to them in Bento and open them automatically. (You can also open them from the Finder.)

If you do not have Adobe Reader to read PDF files, you can download it for free from www.adobe.com. This provides you with another standard format to use to convert your legacy files. It also provides you with a safety net in case your legacy application does not support Save As or Export. In the Print dialog that is used by most applications, you can use the PDF button in the lower left to save the printed output as a PDF file, as shown in Figure 4.3.

Figure 4.3

Save printouts as PDF files.

In most cases, this means that if you can print it, you can save the image as a PDF file and open that with a double-click that launches Adobe Reader if necessary. (Many applications can open PDF files themselves.)

If you are worried about not being able to open old files, converting them to text, RTF, or PDF should solve the problem.

A related issue of file formats arises with media files. You can use Bento's media fields to store images, sounds, and movies. Supported file types include PDF, JPG, TIFF, GIF. MP3, PICT, MOV, and PSD (Photoshop).

If you have an image, sound, or movie that is not in a supported format, you can often use the Export or Save As command to convert it.

Performing a Basic Data Import with CSV Data

This section walks you through the process of importing data either from your own data (current or legacy) or data that you download from the Web. CSV is generally provided as an exportable format from spreadsheets such as Excel or Numbers and databases such as FileMaker Pro.

The data used in this example is from the U.S. Census Bureau; it consists of population projects from 2004 to 2030 as well as the 2000 census data. The data is arranged by state, age, and sex. It consists of 13,572 records, so it provides a good example of a fairly substantial data import. In addition, the data demonstrates some of the issues you need to watch out for when importing data.

NOTE

The data file can be downloaded from the U.S. Census Bureau website (http://www.census.gov) along with a number of other data files. In addition, you can download a ZIP archive of the file from this book's site as described in the introduction. Despite the massive amount of data in the file, the file itself is actually quite small, just 2.3MB; the ZIP archive is 1MB.

In the first release of Bento, data import is limited to comma-separated values (CSV). This is a standard file format for data that separates the data elements with commas. (In some environments, a different separator is used; you can change it in Bento.) CSV data can be numeric or text; it looks like this:

```
red, blue, green
1, 2, 3
hello there, Henry IV, 20,354
```

As you can see, the commas separate the data values. The first thing to check in your data is whether it contains commas that are not separators. For example, in the third line, are there three values (the last one being a number—20,354), or are there four values (the last two being two numbers—20 and 354)?

If data contains embedded commas, you can place the entire value inside quotation marks. There is no ambiguity in this line of data, which contains three (not four) values:

```
Hello there, Henry IV, "20,354"
```

If the data itself contains quotation marks, double them. For example, the first element of this line of data might be a quote that is written

```
"Hello, there"
```

If you want to preserve the quotes, it should be written as

```
""Hello, there""
```

In most cases, you do not have to worry about this problem. If you are working with an application that can export CSV data (such as FileMaker Pro, Numbers, or Excel), all this is done for you automatically.

Another thing Bento handles for you automatically is labeling the data. (This may be an export option in the program you are using.) If you have labels in your file, the first record consists of the names of the fields being exported. If this option is available, use it; it makes your import easier, as you see later in this section.

TIP

Importing into Bento is so fast that you can try your first import without worrying about these issues, provided that you have some way of checking your import. Open the file you are about to import in another application (preferably the one you used to create it). Write down some things to check: the total number of records, the total value of numeric fields, and so forth. Then, try your Bento import and check these values as described later in this chapter. If they match, your import was successful. Conversely, if you do not have values to check against, your import has to be considered as potentially incomplete. If your data does not lend itself to arithmetic sums, you can spot check the data values that have been imported. The two records that are most likely to show import errors are the first and last records. If your field mapping is off (or the quotation marks and commas are off in the input file), you will find half of one record in the second record's fields or vice versa. If all the fields in the last imported record are what they should be, and if the total number of records is correct, you are probably fairly safe. The degree of checking that you need to do depends on the criticality of the data.

The simplest way to import data into Bento is to automatically create a new library. That is the process described here. Begin by choosing File > Import. The Import window shown in Figure 4.4 opens. You can also open it by dragging an import file to the Bento icon into the Source list in the Bento window (Bento 1), or into the Libraries list in the Libraries & Fields pane (Bento 2).

Select the file to import, and, for its destination, select New Library. Provide a name for the library. Bento attempts to open the file and display the first record in the main section of the Import window. In this case, the first record contains field names, and they are displayed. Use the left and right arrows below the data display to move through the file. As you can see from the checkbox beneath the field values, you have an option whether to use the first record as field names.

TIP

As shown at the bottom of Figure 4.4, you can step through the data and choose any record to use as the column names. That record is treated as the first record in the file, and the remaining records are imported. If you select record 5 as the column names, the data import starts with column 6.

In Bento 1, you also have the ability to change the character that separates values within a record. You can use either a comma or semicolon; there is a default value set for your location, and normally that is the one to use. If you are importing a file that was created in another country, it may use a separator other than the one you usually use, so you can change it for the specific import.

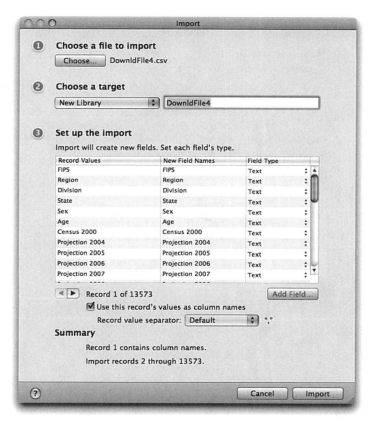

Figure 4.4

Begin to import data.

Step through a few records, as shown in Figure 4.5, to make certain that the data looks correct. Note that the field names picked up from the first (or selected) record in Figure 4.4 are shown next to the data values as you step through each record. If commas or quotation marks are mismatched, you will often see the problem here, and you can correct the import data. Also check the total number of records. If it is off, that, too, is likely a commas or quotation mark issue.

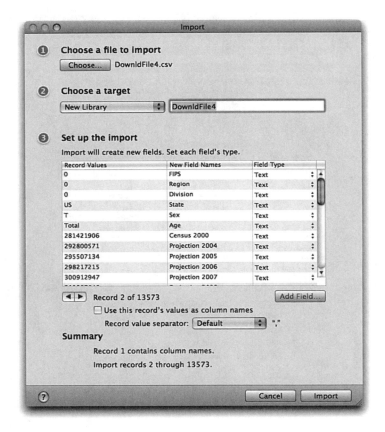

Figure 4.5

Step through the records.

By default, all fields are imported as text. Change the field types to the actual types of the data. Do this based on the field names as well as on the data. For example, data that is organized into tabular form often contains totals and subtotals. These can pose issues that you need to deal with. In the population data, for example, you can easily see that the Age field contains the age of people. However, that does not mean that it is a numeric field.

The Age field sometimes contains the word "Total," as shown in Figure 4.5. In addition, it contains the value 85+ for people 85 or older.

Figure 4.6 shows how you can change the field types. You can also indicate that a field is not to be imported. Remember that the field names and types apply to all records. Changing them in the Import dialog has to be done once—not separately—for each imported record.

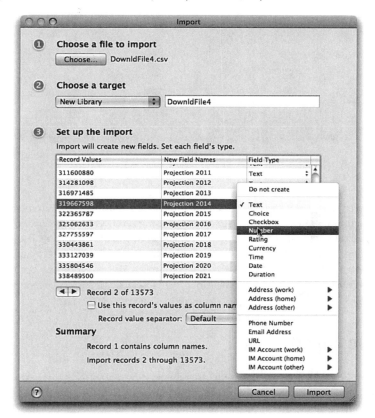

Figure 4.6

Change field types as needed.

Now you are ready to import the data. Bento is very fast. (This data import takes less than a minute.) Bento creates a library for you; you can then use the techniques in the preceding chapters to rearrange the fields and customize it, as shown in Figure 4.7.

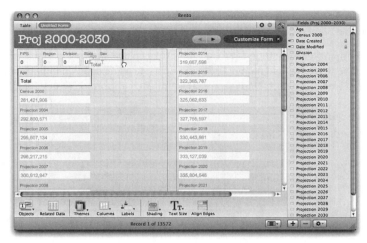

Figure 4.7

Customize the library.

Here is another area where you can check the data import. You can show the Summary Row in table view and total various columns or count the values. You can do this in conjunction with finding subsets of data. This is one of the reasons you need to know what you are importing. This data set (like many) includes total and subtotal rows. That means that the totals of columns are much too high, because they contain basic data as well as totals and subtotals. This is a common occurrence. In fact, there are quite a few anomalies that you may run into. The next section gives you some tips about cleaning up data.

Cleaning Up Imported Data

When you are importing data to Bento or any other destination, you often need to do some cleanup work. It is usually easiest to do the cleanup before the import. This is because if you are using the original program, you have all the tools available to manipulate the data. In addition, the cleaner the data, the fewer import errors you have.

The most basic form of cleanup is to verify the data. Are the phone numbers still valid? Are the names correctly spelled? Of course, while it is desirable to clean up the data as much as possible and as early as possible in the process, this is the real world. One way to handle data importing is to add a new field to the Bento library after you have imported the data. Make it a checkbox field called Verified. Leave the data in its basic state, and, as you use it in Bento, check that it is valid. This means that the data you actually use is cleaned up before the rarely used data. Check the Verified checkbox so that you know you have checked individual data records. Gradually, you will clean up most or even all your data. (And remember that you can find data that is not verified using Advanced Find.)

TIP

A variation on this strategy works for data that can change over time. Instead of a Verified checkbox, create a date field called Last Checked. Whenever you check the data (perhaps by actually using the email address or telephone number), choose Insert > Current Date and Time to update that field.

There is another common cleanup process that's often necessary when importing spreadsheets. Spreadsheets today occupy a place somewhere in the middle of databases (because they support data storage and searching), word processing documents (because you can format them for display and printing), and traditional data tables (rows × columns). The hardest spreadsheets to import are those that are specially formatted to look their best. As you have seen, Bento is happy to import an initial record with field names. But what happens when you have five beautifully formatted rows of text with titles centered (and perhaps with parenthetical comments)?

What happens is that you have to remove all that beautiful formatting and extraneous text so that you have only a single title row (or none at all). Naturally, you should do this in a copy of the original spreadsheet. (To help solve this problem, use the option to select a row other than the literal first row of the table for column names and a location to start importing.)

In the old days, a spreadsheet document consisted of a single sheet. Today, a spreadsheet can have several sheets within it, and formulas can reference all the sheets within a spreadsheet workbook. But old habits die hard, and many spreadsheets have a single set of rows and columns in the upper left and a variety of smaller rows × columns tables (each with its own nicely formatted labels and titles) all over the spreadsheet. The only way to successfully import this data is to split the complex spreadsheet apart into basic rows × columns tables, each with at most a single title row at the top. Or in Bento 2, copy these smaller tables and paste them into a table view.

NOTE

Dealing with these spreadsheets is not really a Bento issue. If you have one of these old spreadsheets, it still functions better as a spreadsheet if you split it apart into separate sheets, each of which is a simple rows × columns table.

Finally, consider cleaning up spreadsheets by removing total and subtotal rows. You can use these values for checking your import, but by stripping the spreadsheet down to its data and removing calculated totals and pretty formatting, you will make your life easier in the long run. (You can also omit them from the import dialog rather than deleting them from the spreadsheet itself.)

Importing Other File Formats

New In Bento 2, you can import a wide range of data formats. In addition to CSV data, you can import data directly from Excel spreadsheet formats, from Numbers, and from tab-delimited files such as those created by AppleWorks. The basic process is the same as importing CSV data.

5

Working with Phone, URL, IM, and Address Fields and Lists in Contacts

IN THIS CHAPTER

■ Exploring the Contacts Library   65

■ Working with Address Fields and Lists   69

■ Adding Address Fields and Lists to Your Forms   72

Exploring the Contacts Library

One of the libraries that comes with Bento is the Contacts library. It lets you store contact information names, addresses (physical, email, and instant messaging—IM), birthdays, job information, and more. As shipped, it provides a powerful personal contacts database, and, as you see in this chapter, much of its functionality is provided by standard Bento data and interface elements that you can easily use in other contexts.

Of course, Bento also ships with libraries that are integrated with your Mac OS X Address Book application. Address Book has even more information than does the Contacts library. Furthermore, it has the enormously important feature of automatically being integrated and synchronized with Address Book as necessary. This synchronization can extend far beyond your computer so that your Address Book data can automatically be synchronized with your MobileMe account, with your other Macs, and with your iPhone, PDA, or other synchronizable device. In fact, by using MobileMe, this synchronization can extend to PCs running Windows.

⊖   You find more on these matters in Chapter 8, "Using Built-In Bento Libraries for Address Book," p. 118.

Starting by exploring the nonintegrated and synchronized Contacts library lets you look at a simple case of real-life Bento use. And there are cases in which the lack of integration and synchronization has its advantages. The most obvious such cases are those in which you need to keep track of contacts that you do not want to mingle with your own contacts. If you are coaching a sports team, managing the membership of an association, or working on a political campaign, it can be important that the data for the team, association, or campaign be kept separate from your own personal data. Furthermore, in some cases, your role as guardian of the contact data may be temporary—perhaps just for the year. Thus, you need a powerful way to organize the data, you need a tool that lets you quickly import last year's data from the person who managed it in the past, and you also need a tool that lets you easily export it in a commonly used format so that next year's data guardian can import it into whatever software on whatever computer he will use. You can use groups in Address Book to organize your contacts, but if you really need separation, nothing beats a completely separate library.

⊖   For more details on importing and exporting data and libraries, see Chapter 15, "Importing and Exporting Bento Data and Libraries," p. 199.

Start your exploration by creating a Contacts library in Bento. Choose File > New Library or click the + button beneath the Source list at the left of the Bento 1 window or beneath the libraries list at the top of the Libraries & Fields pane in Bento 2. This opens the New Library dialog, as shown in Figure 5.1.

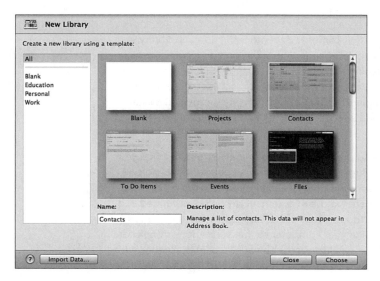

Figure 5.1

Create a new Bento Contacts library.

The Bento library templates are organized into groups (Education, Personal, and Work); some, including the Contacts library, are available from each of the groups.

TIP

In the New Library dialog, libraries with the same name are, indeed, the same libraries no matter which groups they appear in. If they are customized for use in a specific context, they are renamed.

As you explore this dialog, remember that the lower right of the dialog gives you information about each library as you click on it. Also, you can rename the library you are about to create by typing the new name at the lower left of the dialog. Particularly if your Contacts library is to be for a special purpose, consider naming it appropriately right from the start.

When you click the Choose button, Bento creates the new library. As always with a Bento template, a record with simple data is created, as shown in Figure 5.2.

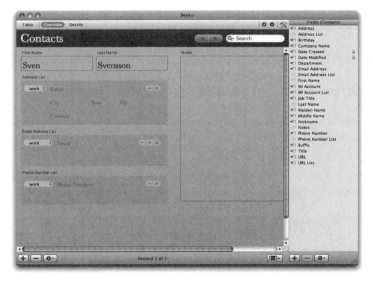

Figure 5.2

Click Choose to create the library.

Whenever you create a library, you have at least two views of the library available from the navigation bar at the top of the Records area: a table view and at least one form view. In the case of the Contacts library, there are two form views. The first one is Overview, shown in Figure 5.2; the second is Details, shown in Figure 5.3.

Figure 5.3

Details form of the Contacts library.

You can create any form views you want, and you can name them whatever you want. There is a logic in the Contacts library that you may want to follow. The table view, the only such view, is always the leftmost view. It allows you to see more than one record at a time. The forms in the Contacts library move into greater details as you move to the right, although you are limited to seeing one record at a time.

New In Bento 2, you can use the split view to show multiple records in the table view at the top and a form view of a single record at the bottom, as shown in Figure 5.4.

Figure 5.4

The Bento 2 split view lets you see multiple records in a table view at the same time as a single record in a form view.

You can rearrange the sequence of the form views in the Bento window simply by dragging their names to the right or left. When you quit Bento or move to another library, Bento remembers which view you were last looking at; the next time you open that library, you will see that same view first.

Working with Address Fields and Lists

The heart of the Contacts library is the address fields and lists for addresses, phone numbers, IM addresses, and email addresses. Bento manages these special-purpose fields and lists for you. In this section, you see how to use them, and in the following section, you see how easily you can create them.

To enter data in any field, just click it, and all editable fields in the library are shown with a background color that is distinct from the background of the form itself; the current field is highlighted, as shown in Figure 5.5.

Figure 5.5
Enter data.

At the left of the Details form, you find lists for addresses, email addresses, phone numbers, and URLs (note the field names above the fields). Although you initially see only one item in each list, you can easily create new items.

Working with Address, Email, Phone Number, and URL List Fields in Bento 1

As shown in Figure 5.5, there is a + button to the right of each item; click it to add a new item. This has just happened in Figure 5.6, and you can see that the scrollbar for the address list is now active because there are now two records.

Figure 5.6

Add a new address.

A – button allows you to remove the visible item from a list. Bento asks you to confirm any list item you attempt to delete. All these lists function exactly the same way, and that behavior is automatic to Bento lists. You are warned before deleting a list item.

In addition to the + and – buttons, sometimes there is a third button to the right of the list item. In Figure 5.7, you can see that you can click an email address to open a new email message in Mail addressed using that email address.

Figure 5.7

Open an outgoing email message from an email address in Bento.

In a list of URLs, you can open a URL in your default browser with a button similar to the send email button shown in Figure 5.7.

Working with Address, Email, Phone Number, and URL List Fields in Bento 2

In Bento 2, the Bento list fields have been slightly redesigned to have a simpler and more consistent interface. Figure 5.8 shows Contacts in Bento 2.

Figure 5.8

Bento 2 list fields have a slightly different interface.

In Bento 2, there are always two buttons at the top-right corner of a list field. The first does something specific to that type of list field. The second opens a contextual menu of commands that can be applied to the specific element of the list. The layout of those menus is always the same:

- The first item is the default action that is also accessible from the left-hand button.

- The last two items add another element to the list or delete the current one.

- Other actions may appear in between.

The default actions for the list elements are

- Map an address.

- Send an email.

- Display a phone number in large type.

- Open the IM account in iChat.

- Open a URL.

In Bento 2, only the address field has additional actions. They are

- Directions To.

- Directions From.

- Copy Mailing Label. (This combines the address elements into a single block of text that you can paste onto an envelope with proper spacing and line breaks.)

NOTE

The mapping and directions actions open Google Maps and fill in the appropriate address automatically.

Adding Address Fields and Lists to Your Forms

If a field is defined as being one of the address types (address, phone number, email address, URL, or IM account), the Fields list in the Bento window shows the field as well as a list for that address type. You can add either or both to your form simply by dragging it (or them) to the Records area. In Figure 5.9, you can see that the Email field defined in the Contacts library has been dragged to the Records area to join the Email list that already was there.

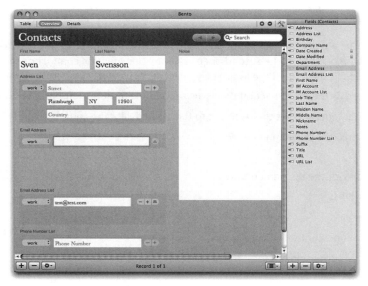

Figure 5.9
As opposed to lists, fields let you see a single address at a time.

If you do this, the field lets you choose from the addresses entered into the list, as shown in Figure 5.10. The Custom command lets you add another label into the list; Other uses the Other label for an unspecified address.

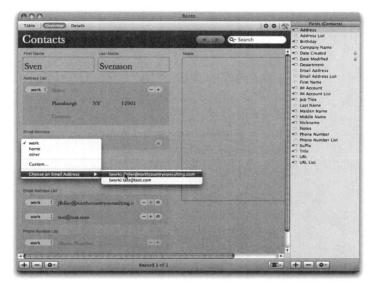

Figure 5.10

In an address field, you can choose from the addresses entered into the corresponding list.

A given address type has only one list. Thus, if you have a URL field called MyURL and another URL field called YourURL, there is a single URL list that contains all the values from both MyURL and YourURL.

With these basic interface building blocks, Bento immediate solves a number of issues that you may have encountered in trying to customize other databases or organizers. Now that the complexities and variations of addresses are off your mind, you can explore how Bento helps you with calculating data. That is the topic of the next chapter.

6

Working with Bento Fields and Calculations

IN THIS CHAPTER

- Exploring the Exercise Log   75

- Creating and Formatting Date Fields in Exercise Log   77

- Creating and Formatting a Number Field in Exercise Log   81

- Creating and Formatting Calculations in Exercise Log   82

- Creating and Formatting Choice Fields   87

- Creating and Formatting Checkbox Fields   88

- Creating and Formatting Currency Fields   89

- Creating and Formatting Automatic Counter Fields   89

- Creating and Formatting Rating Fields   90

- Editing Bento Fields   90

Exploring the Exercise Log

By now, you have seen the basics of Bento: how to use the Bento window, how to create forms, how to import data from a non-Bento file to a new library, and how to work with the built-in Phone, URL, IM, and Address fields and lists. In the course of all this, you have seen the basics of using fields.

This chapter covers most of the Bento field types in detail, showing how a number of them can be used in Exercise Log and providing information about others as well. However, some Bento field types are described in other chapters.

↪ Phone, URL, IM, and Address fields together with their associated lists are discussed in Chapter 5, "Working with Phone, URL, IM, and Address Fields and Lists in Contacts," page 69.

↪ Media fields are discussed in Chapter 7, "Expanding the Inventory Library with Related Records and Collections," p. 93 in the section, "Exploring the Inventory Library."

↪ Related records list fields are discussed in Chapter 7, "Expanding the Inventory Library with Related Records and Collections," p. 101.

⊖   Message list fields are discussed in Chapter 10, "Working with Bento's Projects Library to Use Related Records from iCal Tasks, iCal Events, and Address Book," p. 146 in the section, "Working with Related Records from Mail."

⊖   File List fields are discussed in Chapter 13, "Organizing a Group Project with Bento," p. 181, in the section, "Add a File List Field."

Exercise Log is one of the built-in Bento libraries. You can see the basic library in Figure 6.1.

Figure 6.1

Explore the Exercise Log library.

This library provides a simple way to track your exercise routine. You can expand it with some new fields that make it a bit more useful (and that demonstrate features of Bento fields in the process).

In the basic library, you enter all the data, including the calories burned and the duration of the exercise. With a little effort, you can modify it so that calories burned and duration are both calculated.

To do this calculation, you need to add two fields:

- You need to enter a stop time field so that you can calculate the duration.

- You also need to know how many calories are burned for a given unit of time for the exercise that you are doing. Given that number, you can then multiply it by the calculated duration to compute the number of calories burned. This field can be called calorie rate.

There is a simple reason why these changes can improve the library (other than providing an example of how to use fields and calculations). Calculating the duration from a start and stop time is a simple calculation, and it is one that occasionally trips up people when they do it manually. With Bento, you can enter a time by clicking the clock next to a time field or by clicking the calendar next to a date field. (You see the difference later in this chapter.) By default, the current date and time are entered, and there is little room for error. Of course, that means you need access to Bento when you start and stop your exercise; without such immediate access, you can still click the clock or calendar and easily make the adjustment for the current start or stop time.

When it comes to calculating the calories burned, that, too, is not a particularly onerous task if you do it by hand. However, if you can do everything automatically after the start and stop times are entered, the margin for error is greatly reduced. (Often these simple steps generate careless errors.)

And as if that were not enough, if the calories burned per unit of time is entered into a field on the form, that value is constant for each record that uses the same type of exercise. You can just duplicate the record and change the start and stop times to have everything properly updated.

To complete the process, in addition to adding the stop time and calorie rate, you need to make the duration and calories burned fields into calculations. To do this, you can create new calculation fields and remove the old entry fields.

Creating and Formatting Date Fields in Exercise Log

In Chapter 1, "Bento: The Database for the Rest of Us," you saw the variety of fields that you can create in Bento; in Chapter 3, "Working with Bento Forms," you saw how to change the look of a library. In this section, you find a step-by-step walkthrough of both processes as you create the two new fields for the stop time and calories burned per hour (calorie rate).

Creating a Stop Date Field

The Exercise Log library has a time field for you to enter the time you start the exercise. That makes sense: time fields are for time values. But frequently if you are entering times that will delineate a period of time (rather than a specific time such as an appointment), you may not want to use the time field. Rather, you can use a date field that has the option of including month, day, year, as well as time. This makes the calculation of a duration unambiguous even if the period of time spans one or more days. Although it is unlikely that you will be running for more than a day, it is quite possible that you might be exercising at night, possibly across the midnight break from one day to another. By using a date field, you do not have to worry. (If your exercise happens to take you over the International Date Line, you will be on your own regardless of what field type you use.)

Create a Stop field by clicking the + at the bottom of the Fields list or by choosing Insert > New Field. The dialog shown in Figure 6.2 opens.

This dialog lets you choose any of the field types you want. The buttons at the lower right let you create such a field and continue to create another field, close the dialog without saving anything, or create the single field and close the dialog so you can continue with what you were doing.

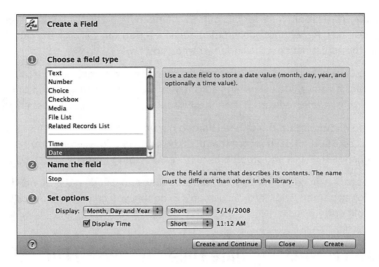

Figure 6.2

Create a date field for Stop.

Date fields let you set various display options, as shown in Figure 6.2. You can choose from Month, Day, and Year or just Month and Day. You can also choose the level of detail. As you change these options, the sample data shown in Figure 6.2 changes. The detail options for dates when Month, Day, and Year are displayed are

- **Short**: 10/25/2008

- **Medium**: Oct 25, 2008

- **Long**: October 25, 2008

- **Full**: Saturday, October 25, 2008

The sequence of Month, Day, and Year is determined by your International settings in System Preferences—specifically the Formats pane.

For times, there are only two formatting choices: Short contains hour and minutes, whereas Medium adds seconds to the display.

For the Exercise Log, make certain that you set the options at the bottom of the dialog so that both the date and time are visible.

Now, drag the Stop field from the Fields list into the library.

Creating a Start Date Field

If you are following this procedure, you need to do the same to create a new Start field that is a date, not a time field. To do this, you first need to select the existing Start field and delete it. Then, create a new Start field that is a date just as you did with the Stop field. Because it is the same as the Stop field, you can also select the Stop field in the Fields list, duplicate it, and then change the name from the default Stop 1 to Start.

As you drag each field, you see it travel beneath your mouse; it also shows up in the place where Bento places it so you can drop it in the exact location you want.

Using Date and Time Field Controls

Date and Time fields have small calendar and clock icons to their right, which we get into in this section. Before moving on, however, make sure you check that the fields are properly formatted so that there is space for these icons. Figure 6.3 shows how you can drag the right side of a field to adjust its width; Bento displays a guide when you are in the right position. Before moving on, click the calendar to enter a date and time. If the field is not wide enough, enlarge both Start and Stop fields so the text can be accommodated.

Figure 6.3

Resize the fields if necessary.

From the user's point of view, these controls provide fast data entry. Figure 6.4 shows the calendar in action for a date field.

Figure 6.4

The calendar in action.

You open the calendar by clicking the small calendar icon next to a date field. Then, you can navigate through the calendar using either the number at the top and the up and down arrows, or the arrows at the upper right. To select a date, you click on it. If you then close the calendar, that date is placed in the associated field. Alternatively, double-click the date you want; the calendar closes, and the date is entered in the field.

The process is similar for time fields. Figure 6.5 shows how you can set the time: with up and down arrows for a selected hour, minute, or am/pm field, by typing into those fields, or by dragging the hands of the clock.

Figure 6.5

Set time values.

Finally, for a date field that includes the option for time, a composite tool is automatically provided, as shown in Figure 6.6.

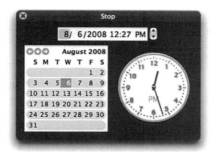

Figure 6.6

A composite date/time field in action.

Creating and Formatting a Number Field in Exercise Log

You now need to create a Calories Rate field that will be used in calculating the calories burned for your exercise time. This number field will contain the rate at which calories are burned per hour for this exercise.

You can work from the sample data in the Exercise Log library, which shows 1,400 calories burned in one hour of exercising. To start, you can use this value, but you should check any of the various exercise calculators you can find on the Web (search for "calorie rate counter") because the true value depends on the specific exercise as well as your body weight.

After you have created your field, drag it into the form. Figure 6.7 shows how you create a number field.

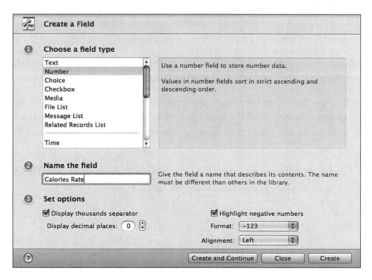

Figure 6.7

Create a number field.

Your options are shown at the bottom of the dialog. You can choose whether to display a thousands separator (what it is depends on your International settings in System Preferences) and how many decimal places to use. Note that these are for display of the data in the field. If you choose not to display a thousands separator and type in 123,456,789, Bento accepts it and displays it as 123456789.

If you choose to highlight negative numbers, they are shown in red. You can also choose a format for negative numbers: –123 or (123). Finally, you can choose whether the number (positive or negative) is aligned to the right or left of the field. In general, when numbers are displayed vertically, right alignment looks best because that is how people normally write them and use them when they are adding them up.

Creating and Formatting Calculations in Exercise Log

Bento calculation fields let you create calculations that combine data in other fields with constants (unchanging values such as pi) and with changing but known values outside Bento databases (such as the current date). You can also create calculations or formulas inside spreadsheet cells and inside fields of databases such as FileMaker Pro or Access. Some of those formulas can become complex; they can even include major programming techniques such as transfers of control (if/then statements, for example), temporary variables, and more.

Bento's calculations are powerful and simple. If you are used to thinking in procedural terms (do this, then that, then the other thing…), Bento calculations are different. Like Bento libraries (and databases in general), they describe a formula or relationship that is evaluated as needed from the data at hand.

Working with the Calculation Dialog

In this section, you see how to create two calculation fields based on the fields in the Exercise Log as modified previously in this chapter. First, you should become familiar with the Calculation dialog. When you create a new field, you can choose its type, as shown in Figure 6.2.

Next, you see the Calculation dialog that lets you name the field (just as you always do), specify the calculation, and set the type of the result, as shown in Figure 6.8.

As always, Bento attempts to convert fields of one type to another as needed. In Bento and any other database, it is best to use the most specific type for a given field. You can store dates in text fields, for example, but only date fields can take advantage of Bento's automatic date formatting and simplified date entry.

In the lower left of the dialog shown in Figure 6.8, you can click Show Examples. This flips the dialog to its back, and you see examples of calculations, as shown in Figure 6.9.

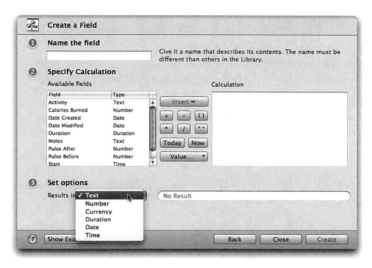

Figure 6.8

Name the field and set its result type.

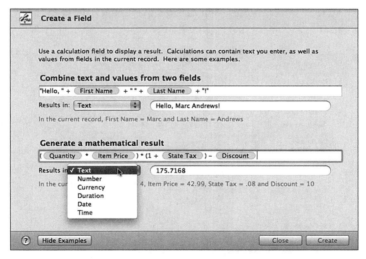

Figure 6.9

Experiment with Bento calculation examples.

This dialog is live: you can modify the text in the two calculations and see the result in the field just below each of the two calculations. You can also adjust the result's type so that you can see how Bento changes the result.

Flip the dialog back to the front by clicking Hide Examples. Now you are ready to create your calculation fields.

Creating the Duration Field

The Exercise Log library has a Duration field into which you can type the duration of your exercise using the standard Bento duration symbols (h/hour, m/minutes, s/seconds—even the most ardent exercise is unlikely to need d/day in the Duration field, but it is there if necessary).

Now that you have both a Start and Stop field in the library, you can create a new Duration field that is a calculation. Delete the existing Duration field, and begin to create a new one: click the + at the bottom of the Fields list or choose Insert > New Field. Select Calculation for the field type.

> ### NOTE
>
> Now that you have created a number of fields, the details of using the + at the bottom of the Fields list or Insert > New Field are omitted for the balance of the book.

The simplest way to create a calculation is to select each field in the calculation in turn from the list and either double-click or then click Insert to move it into the calculation area at the right. Where necessary, click one of the operators. You can also type into the calculation area or use a combination of typing and clicking. You can specify the result type of the calculation in the lower left.

As you create the calculation, Bento attempts to evaluate it and places the result at the lower right of the dialog. Figure 6.10 shows the process as the calculation is being built. Because it is not yet complete, you are warned at this moment that it cannot be evaluated.

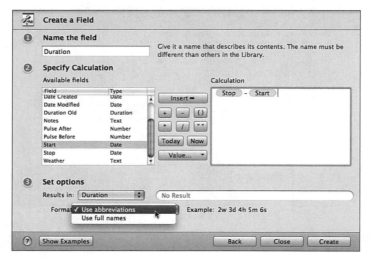

Figure 6.10

Create the calculation.

If the fields contain data, you can see the actual result, as shown in Figure 6.11. If you do not have data in the fields of the current record, click Create to create the field and then enter some data in the Start and Stop fields. (You can use the calendar icons to quickly select the current date and time for each. You may want to move the Start time value back an hour or two to make the duration calculation more significant.)

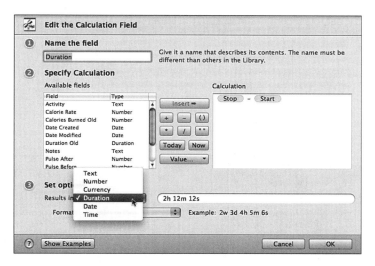

Figure 6.11

Bento evaluates the calculation based on data in the current record.

Bento stores all dates and times in seconds. If you change the result type of this calculation to a number, you see the number of seconds in the duration. For this set of data, the numeric value is 7,932:

- 2 hours = 120 minutes = 7,200 seconds
- 12 minutes = 720 seconds
- 12 seconds

Complete the process of creating the Duration field by dragging the new field from the Fields list into the form. Check the format setting (Shading and Text Size) of Duration Old to make certain that the new field's settings match. Experiment by entering some data into the new Start and Stop fields. The Duration field should update automatically.

Creating the Calories Burned Field

Now that you have the new Duration field created as a calculation and you have the Calorie Rate field created as a number, you can create the main calculation: Calories Burned. Before creating the field, make certain that you have a value entered in the new Calorie Rate field. To make your testing as simple as possible, adjust the Start and Stop fields to be exactly one hour apart. For Calorie Rate, enter 1,400 (the value the sample record has in the built-in library).

> **NOTE**
>
> Whether you use a comma is up to you: Bento is equally happy with 1400 and 1,400.

Now create a Calories Burned calculation field. With those values, you can enter a calculation of Calorie Rate * Duration, as shown in Figure 6.12.

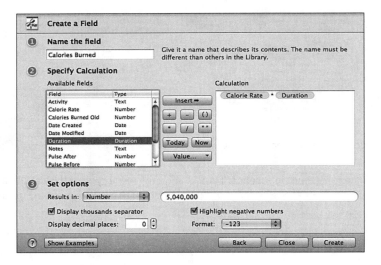

Figure 6.12

Create the Calories Burned calculation.

Here is one of the areas in which Bento's live calculation helps you. The result of the calculation is over 5 million calories, a number that is obviously too high. Remember that Bento is using seconds to store dates and times. You have entered 1,400 as the number of calories burned per hour, but the duration is calculated in seconds. You could require that the arithmetic be done before data is entered, but why not let Bento do it? There are 3,600 seconds in an hour (60 minutes * 60 seconds). If you divide the Duration field by 3,600, the calculation will be correct, as shown in Figure 6.13.

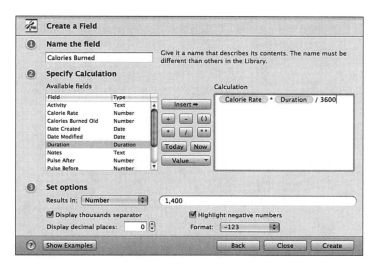

Figure 6.13

Complete the calculation.

Creating and Formatting Choice Fields

Choice fields are displayed in a popup menu. The user can select a single value from that menu. When you create the choice field, you must provide at least one choice. You can use – for a choice on a line by itself which creates a separator in the popup menu. Figure 6.14 shows how to set the choice values. You can select a row and use + or – to add a new row beneath it or to delete it. You can also click directly on a line and enter a value. To rearrange the choices, just click one and drag it up or down to its new position.

Choice fields work best when the number of choices is less than 20. (Some interface designers would suggest a dozen as a maximum.) If you have more choices, you have to scroll through too many values to find what you want and even to know what is available. You can minimize this problem by arranging the choices in groups with separators, but you might want to consider using a text field with the type-ahead option so that as you type, previously entered values are shown.

Now your modified Exercise Log calculates duration and calories burned. Along the way, you have seen how to use calculations and how to use Date, Time, and Date/Time fields. The balance of this chapter explores other commonly used fields in Bento.

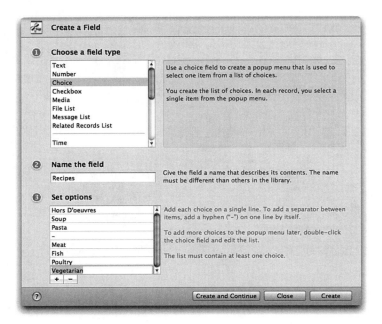

Figure 6.14

Enter choice values.

Creating and Formatting Checkbox Fields

A checkbox field consists of a checkbox and some text, which is the field name. Examples are status information such as Verified, Completed, or In Progress. Bento checkboxes have a slightly different functionality than other checkboxes because you can either check a checkbox or not check it: The values are Yes and No. Sometimes that Yes/No structure does not fit the data easily. For example, if you want to keep track of gender, you can use a choice field with values Male and Female. If you use a checkbox field, you would have to name it either Male or Female. The records checked would be Male (or Female), and the other gender would consist of any record that is not checked.

Status, too, often lends itself to a choice field so that you can change it from Not Started to In Progress to Completed. If you use a checkbox, you work with the single value (such as Finished).

> **NOTE**
>
> Choice and checkbox fields are good ways of storing data, but they are also excellent ways of organizing data. You can search your library for a specific checkbox value to limit the records you are looking at (Not Finished, for example). In Chapter 7, "Expanding the Inventory Library with Related Records and Collections," you see how you can use a checkbox or choice field to drive the whole process of maintaining a Smart Collection.

Creating and Formatting Currency Fields

Currency fields are a special type of number field. You set them up as shown in Figure 6.15. You can choose the currency symbol to use. In Figure 6.15, you can see that the currently selected value is the Zimbabwe Dollars (a Z). When the mouse is released, the symbol changes to the Euro (€).

The checkbox to show all regions provides you with a much longer list of currency symbols (and is an example of how lengthy choice fields can be problematic).

As with number fields, if you highlight negative numbers, they are shown in color. Also, as with number fields, you can align the currency value left or right.

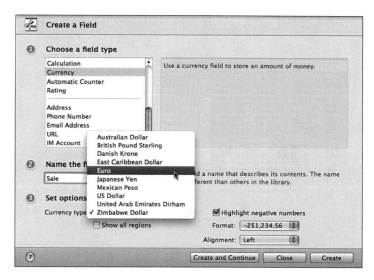

Figure 6.15

Set options for a currency field.

Creating and Formatting Automatic Counter Fields

An automatic counter is used to provide a number for each record. You specify the number to be used for the next record and the increment to be used, and Bento takes care of everything.

For example, if you start at 1 with an increment of 1, the automatic counter fields for the first 5 records are 1, 2, 3, 4, and 5. If you start at 20 with an increment of 5, the values are 20, 25, 30, and so forth.

In many databases, it is critically important to have primary keys with unique values that you can use in creating relationships. In Bento, the entire mechanism of relationships is managed for you without having to create keys, so you do not have to worry about it.

Creating and Formatting Rating Fields

Finally, you can create a rating field. You give it a name and indicate the rating values to be used—you can go up to 10. Then, as shown in Figure 6.16 in the upper right, dots appear for the values, and you can click on a dot to indicate the rating. For example, the Popularity field is a rating field that allows five values; in Figure 6.16, the third dot was clicked and three stars are shown.

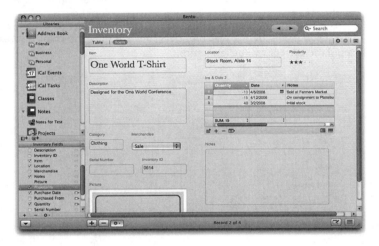

Figure 6.16
Use a rating field.

Editing Bento Fields

You can change the name of a field and change its options by double-clicking it in the Fields list. Or you can choose Edit from the Actions icon below the Fields list in Bento 2. This can be particularly useful with choice fields: you can change the contents of the choice field's popup menu in this way, as shown in Figure 6.17.

If you delete a choice, as shown here, those values remain in the field. So if you have a record in which second floor is selected (that is the choice about to be deleted), those values remain. In the popup menu displaying choice values for those records, second floor is still visible. It is not visible in other records.

New An important new feature in Bento 2 is the capability to change field types. Figure 6.18 shows one of the Bento Quickies from Chapter 17, "Bento Quickies." It lets you keep track of software serial numbers. Because serial numbers often include letters, that field is a text field. With the Serial Number field selected, you can convert a text field into almost any other type of simple field. (You cannot convert it to one of the list fields, to a media field, or to a calculation.)

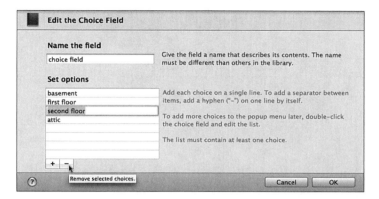

Figure 6.17

Edit a choice field.

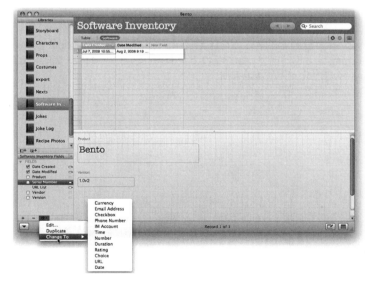

Figure 6.18

Change the type of a text field.

In table view, you can use the triangle at the right of a column header to access all available commands for that field: they include changing its type, as shown in Figure 6.19.

Figure 6.19

Change a field's type in table view.

You can generally change any field type to text, and you can change a text field to any other type. Some conversions may be a two-step process, such as Date to Text and then Text to Rating. In the process, Bento may warn you about data loss.

7

Expanding the Inventory Library with Related Records and Collections

IN THIS CHAPTER

■ Exploring the Inventory Library 93

■ Creating a Library from Scratch 96

■ Using Relationships to Track Inventory 98

■ Using Collections 107

■ Using Smart Collections 109

Exploring the Inventory Library

Just as Exercise Log was used in the last chapter to demonstrate the use of various Bento fields, the Inventory library is used in this chapter to explore concepts of related records and collections. Inventory is one of the built-in Bento libraries. In its basic state, it lets you keep track of inventory items. You can see the basic library in Figure 7.1.

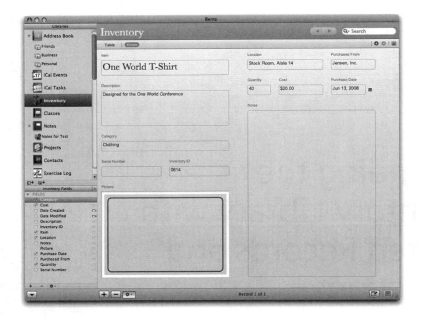

Figure 7.1

Explore the Inventory library.

Using the Inventory library, you can enter the name, price, codes, and so forth. In the lower left of the form shown in Figure 7.1, you can add an image or video clip of the product. This is a standard Bento media field. As you have seen with fields such as the date and time fields, Bento automatically provides interface tools for media fields. For example, when you click in an empty media field, you see the controls shown in Figure 7.2. These controls let you either insert an existing file or, if you have a built-in iSight camera, you can take a picture right on the spot that Bento adds to the field.

When a picture is in the field, the controls shown in Figure 7.3 are available. You can save the picture to disk, change its size, or fit it to the frame.

There are some similarities between the Inventory library and Exercise Log library that was used as an example in Chapter 6, "Working with Bento Fields and Calculations." In both cases, you can enter data directly into the libraries. And, in both cases, you can make data entry much simpler by using some of Bento's features. In the preceding chapter, you saw how calculation fields could help.

In this chapter, you see how you can use another Bento feature to simplify data entry. The target in this chapter is the Quantity field: rather than entering the quantity in the field, you can set up the Inventory library so that you can enter additions and subtractions to the quantity on hand as you buy more inventory and sell items. At first, you might think that this is another calculation, but a calculation requires that you have the component elements available in each database record. (Although elements that are constants or predefined values such as today's date obviously do not need to be present in the record.)

Figure 7.2

Use the media field.

Figure 7.3

Control the media field.

What you need is another library with its own set of records that record the additions and subtractions to your inventory ("ins and outs," as some people call them). Then you need to be able to *relate* that library to the Inventory library. If you have ever done this in a traditional database, you know that it isn't particularly difficult. You just set up a field in one table that matches with a field in the other table and then fill in the proper values, making certain that they remain synchronized... .

It's easier in Bento.

Creating a Library from Scratch

The first step is to create a new library for the Ins and Outs—the additions to and subtractions from inventory. For Ins & Outs, you need three fields:

- Quantity in or out (in is positive numbers, out is negative numbers). This is a number field.

- Date of the transaction. This is a date field.

- Notes about the transaction such as "sold at farmers' market," "bought from co-op," and so forth. This is a text field.

Creating a new library from scratch is slightly different in Bento 1 and Bento 2.

In Bento 1, create a new library from the Blank template and call it Ins & Outs. You may not have created a library from scratch before: if you start from a template, you have a form and sample record along with the basic fields. With a blank library, all you have are the two default fields (Date Created and Date Modified) along with a table and an untitled form—neither of which has any fields in it.

Create the three fields by clicking + at the bottom of the Fields list for each one; set the appropriate name and field type as described in the previous chapter. You can use the Create & Continue button to move on to the next field you want to create, as shown in Chapter 6, Figure 6.7.

Figure 7.4 shows the Ins & Outs library with the fields created. They have been added to the table view.

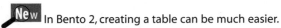 In Bento 2, creating a table can be much easier.

The first step is the same: create a new library from the Blank template and call it Ins & Outs. You are in table view with the two default fields created, as shown in Figure 7.5.

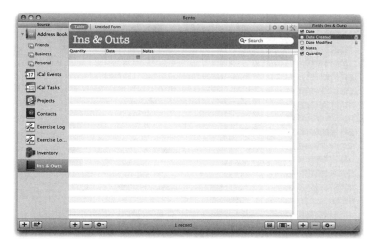

Figure 7.4

Create Ins & Outs in Bento 1.

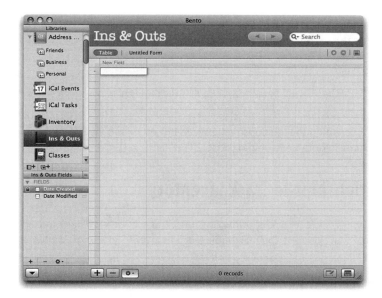

Figure 7.5

Create Ins & Outs in Bento 2.

Double-click the header for the first column that is set by default to New Field. As soon as you click in that header, its name immediately changes to Field 1. At the same time, a new column titled New Field is provided to the right so that you can enter the next field. Just type into the header to change Field 1 to Quantity. Use the triangle next to the name to change the field's type to number, as shown in Figure 7.6.

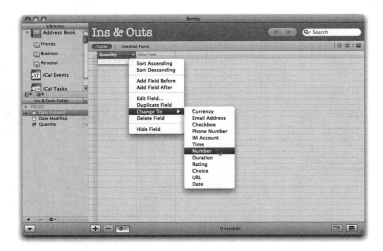

Figure 7.6
Edit the field to make it a number.

Repeat the process for Date and Notes. In the case of notes, you do not have to edit the field: The default field type is text, which is what you want.

TIP

You can still use the process described for Bento 1, but this process is much faster.

The mechanism for creating the relationship between Inventory and Ins & Outs is the next step in the process. It is the same in both Bento 1 and Bento 2.

Using Relationships to Track Inventory

There are several ways to create a relationship in Bento. This section walks you through each of them. All of them assume that you have the main table (such as Inventory) and the table that you will relate to it (Ins & Outs).

Dragging the Related Library onto the Form

You can create a relationship by dragging the library to be related into a form of the main library. Open the Inventory library, select the form, and then drag Ins & Outs from the Source list (Bento 1) or Libraries list (Bento 2) onto the form, as shown in Figure 7.7.

When you release the mouse button, the relationship is created (see Figure 7.8). You see a small table view in the form.

By default, the fields in the related records list are those that are in the table view of the related library, but you can add others or remove this from the related records list view if you want.

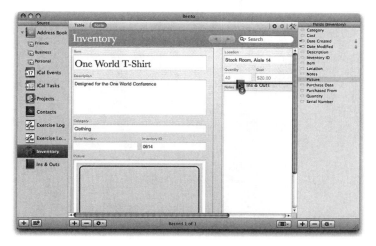

Figure 7.7

Create a relationship by dragging a library onto a form.

Also, a related records list field is created; you see it in the Fields list. In Bento 1, that field is shown in alphabetical order in the Fields list, as shown in Figure 7.8.

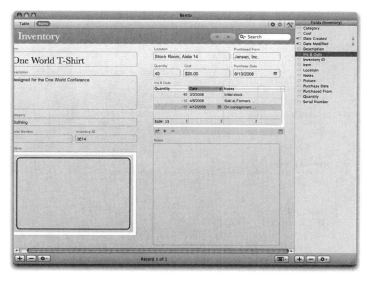

Figure 7.8

Bento creates the relationship.

New In Bento 2, the Fields list at the bottom of the Libraries & Panes list is rearranged. Instead of related records list fields being inserted in the list in alphabetical order, the list is separated into the library's own fields at the top and a list of related data at the bottom, as shown in Figure 7.9.

Figure 7.9

Bento 2 separates related data from local fields in the Fields list.

Adding a Related Records List Field

Alternatively, you can add a related records list field, as shown in Figure 7.10.

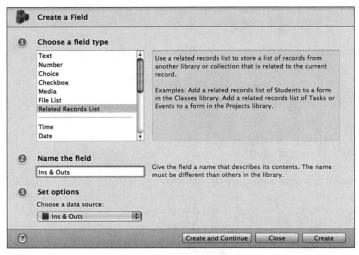

Figure 7.10

Create a related records list field.

If you use this approach, the related records list field is created in the Fields list, and you can then add it to your form as you would any other field.

Formatting the Related Records List Field

You can format the related records list field much like any other field (although you cannot change its text size). One special formatting feature is important to use such a field properly. If you click in the related records list field, the Fields list changes to show the fields from the related library, as shown in Figure 7.11. You can compare this to Figure 7.9, in which a row in the related records list field is highlighted, but the field itself is not active because you have not clicked in it. Click the fields in the Fields list that you want to be shown in the related records list field, just as you would to specify the fields for a table view. To rearrange the fields, just drag the column headers back and forth until they are in the order you want. You can also resize the columns.

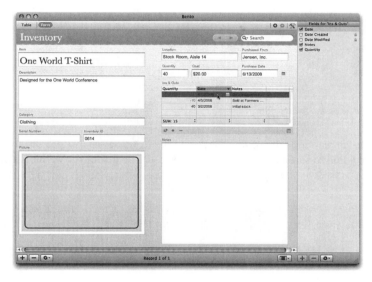

Figure 7.11
Select the fields to be shown in the related records list field.

In Bento 2, there is a small button at the lower right of a related records list field that you can use to switch between the view of fields shown in Figure 7.9 and the view of the fields in the related data, as shown in Figure 7.12.

Figure 7.12

Switch between local fields and related data in Bento 2.

Furthermore, you can rearrange the columns just as in Bento 1, but you can also use the triangle at the top of each column to sort a column or hide it just as you do in table view. This is shown in Figure 7.13.

Figure 7.13

Column headers in related records list fields work the same as they do in table view in Bento 2.

Summarizing a Related Records List Field

At the lower right of a related records list field is the button to show or hide the summary row. Just as you can with a table, you can choose from sum, average, and other functions. Show the summary row and select Sum for the summary function of the quantity column. (If it is not shown in the related records list field, click in the field and click the checkbox in the Fields list for the related library next to Quantity.)

Adding Data to a Related Records List Field

Now you are ready to start using the related records. Enter some data, as shown in Figure 7.14. The related records list field has a vertical scrollbar that is activated as necessary. To add a record, just type in the first blank row. You can also use the + at the lower left of the related records field to add a row. Use the – to delete the selected row.

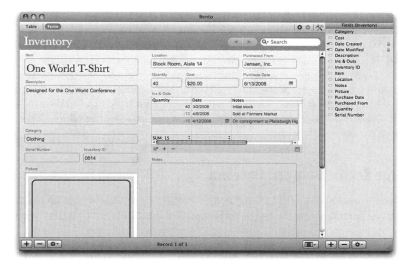

Figure 7.14
Enter data in the related library.

Notice that as you enter the data, the summary row is updated with the ins (positive numbers) and outs (negative numbers). Instead of the static Quantity field in the built-in template, you now have a live inventory tracker.

Reviewing the Related Records

If you go to the Ins & Outs library, you will see that the records you have entered through the related records list in Inventory are in the Ins & Outs library. While you are in the Ins & Outs library, try adding another record to it. Then go back to the Inventory library, where you will see that the new record you added to Ins & Outs is not shown in the related records list field in Inventory.

The reason this new record isn't shown in the related records list is that the only records from Ins & Outs shown in that list field are those that were entered through that Inventory record: they are the related records. If you go to another Inventory record, the related records list field only shows the Ins & Outs records that were entered through the second Inventory record. Bento keeps track of all this so that everything works as it should and you do not have to worry about it.

↪   This will be pursued further in Chapter 13, "Organizing a Group Project with Bento," p. 177.

Bento keeps track of which records in the related library are related to which other library and to which record in the library. Records entered through Inventory show up in the full Ins & Outs library as well as in the Inventory related records list field of the record through which they were entered. You can relate a given library to any number of other records. In addition to Inventory, you might create a library called Production that keeps track of your manufacturing of items. You can relate Ins & Outs to Production as well as Inventory.

WARNING

If you delete a record from Ins & Outs—the basic library that is related to Inventory, Production, and maybe other libraries—that record is deleted everywhere. It is the basic library that stores the data; everything else stores references to the data, and if the data is gone, that is the end of it. A warning dialog appears when you are about to do this, but even the most experienced users occasionally delete records that are needed in related tables. That is why Bento backups are so important.

Improving the Relationship and the Form

You can remove the old Quantity field from the Inventory library to clean things up because it is no longer needed: the summary row shows the current sum of Ins & Outs which is the dynamic quantity on hand.

While you are thinking about removing the Quantity field, take a look at the other fields in that part of the form: Purchased From, Cost, and Purchase Date. You already have a date field in the Ins & Outs related record. The notes field can be used to store the purchased from information, or you can add a Purchased From field to Ins & Outs. If you also add a Cost field to Ins & Outs, you have all the information in this section of the Inventory form, and you are able to store multiple values reflecting costs and suppliers for a variety of purchases.

If you add these fields to Ins & Outs, they are not automatically added to the related records list field. However, you can use the same process you used in setting up the related records list field to add them. Select the related records list field, and the Fields list changes to show the fields in Ins & Outs. (Or in Bento 2, click the icon at the lower right of the related records list field to show the related data.) Click the checkboxes next to the items you want to have displayed and then rearrange and resize the columns.

With those fields removed, you can rearrange the form, as shown in Figure 7.15.

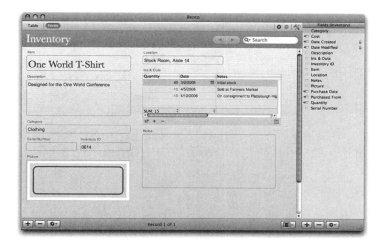

Figure 7.15

Rearrange the form.

The arrangement of fields in Figure 7.15 is one that can be very useful as you build your Bento forms. On the left side of the form is information about the inventory item (a T-shirt in this case). On the right side of the form, the related records list shows information about a number of related records that record purchases and sales. Separating the constant data for the item from the related records can make it easier to use the form.

You might have several sets of related records. In addition to Ins & Outs, you might have a list of vendors for the item; you might also have a list of colors or sizes in which the item is available. There is no limit to the number of related records lists you can have in a Bento library.

There are a few restrictions on the use of related records list fields, though. One is that the visible fields for a given related records list apply to all occurrences of that field. If the related records list field is shown on several forms, all the fields for that related records list show the fields set on any of the forms.

TIP

As you start to add relationships to your Bento libraries, although Bento handles relationships quite simply, you need to remember what the relationships are. Building a number of relationships might make your Bento library harder for you to use. And remember, too, that relationships in Bento are always one step long. If you have a library called A that is related to a library called B, creating a relationship from a new library to A creates no relationship to B.

New In Bento 2, an icon at the bottom of the related records list field lets you go to the record you have clicked on, as shown in Figure 7.16. It opens in the last display you used for the related data—be it the table view or one of the form views.

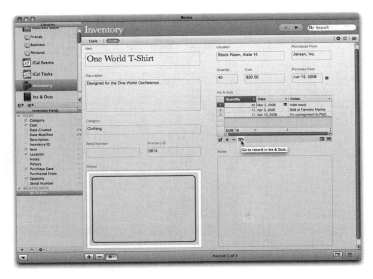

Figure 7.16

Go to a related record in Bento 2.

Once you have gone to the related record, a back button appears in the navigation bar that lets you return to the original record, as shown in Figure 7.17.

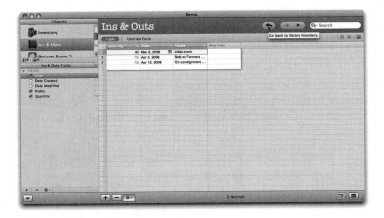

Figure 7.17

Return to the original record in Bento 2.

Using Collections

When you have established a related records list in any of the ways described in the preceding section, Bento keeps track of the appropriate related records. Bento also lets you organize records within a single library into a *collection*. A collection is just that: a subset of records from a single library. Collections are shown in the Source list under their main library. You can expand or contract the main library to see its collections, as shown in Figure 7.18.

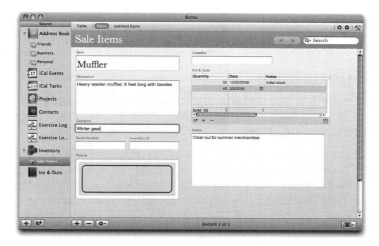

Figure 7.18

Create collections.

In some ways, a collection is similar to a relationship. The reason is that all the items in a collection are actually part of the main library. The collection is a reference to certain records. After you have created a collection, you can add a record to it, and that record shows up in the main library (which is actually where it is stored). If you delete it from the library, it is deleted from the collection. If you delete it from the collection, a dialog lets you choose whether to delete it from both the collection and main library or just from the collection.

The rules for collections are much like those for relationships:

- You can have any number of collections within a library.
- The same record can be in any number of collections within a library.

In the example shown in Figure 7.18, a collection has been set up for Sale Items from Inventory. You can see it in the Source list at the left directly underneath its parent library and slightly indented. You can use the disclosure triangle for the parent library to show or hide its collection. The Sale Items records are still in the Inventory table, but they are collected together. Other such collections might be new items, discontinued items, and so forth. Using collections provides a further way of organizing your Bento data.

Creating an Empty Collection

The simplest way to create a new collection is to choose File > New Collection or to use the Add Collection button from the bottom of the Sources list in Bento 1. It is the second button from the left, just next to the + button. In Bento 2, it is beneath the Libraries list at the top of the Libraries & Fields pane. There, too, it is the second button from the left. Figure 7.19 shows the Add Library button at the left and then the Add Collection button. Note that the icon is slightly different in Bento 2 than in Bento 1.

This action creates a new collection inside the main library. Whether you have selected the main library itself (Inventory in this case) or another collection within it, the collection is created. All collections for a library are placed under its name; you can rearrange them by dragging them up or down.

Adding a Record to a Collection

When you have a collection, you can add records to it. Select the collection and click the Add Record button from the Records area or choose Records > New Record; this adds a record to the collection and, of course, to the main library as well.

If you already have a record, you can add it to any collection within that library. Navigate to the record and choose Add to Collection from the Additional Commands button, as shown in Figure 7.19. (You can also choose Edit > Add To to select the collection to which you want to add it.) If you choose multiple records from a table view, you can add all of them at once to a collection in the same way.

Figure 7.19

Add a record to a collection.

Creating a Collection from Selected Records

You can combine both steps if you want to create a collection from a set of records that you have selected. Select the records in table view or navigate to the specific record from which you want to create a collection. Then choose New Collection from Selection. You are prompted to name the collection, and then it is created. After that, you can manually add records to the collection as described in the previous section.

Using Smart Collections

Collections are a simple way to organize your data in any way that you want. But Bento also provides you with *Smart Collections*. This is the same type of Smart technology that you see in the Finder with Smart Folders and in a variety of other places in Mac OS X.

A Smart Collection consists of an Advanced Find query that selects certain records. The Smart Collection always displays the records that satisfy that query: you do not have to do anything to update the Smart Collection. If a new record's data qualifies it for the Smart Collection, it is part of the Smart Collection. If a change to the record's data disqualifies it, it disappears from the Smart Collection, but it remains in the main library unless you delete it.

 Smart Collections are based on Advanced Find. This is described in detail in Chapter 2, "Using the Bento Window," p. 31.

There are two ways of creating a Smart Collection. If you are working with an Advanced Find, the Save button at the upper right of the window creates a Smart Collection based on that query. Click Save and then enter a name for the Smart Collection, and you're set.

Alternatively, you can choose File > New Smart Collection. This opens Advanced Find so that you can create the query and then click Save.

Here is an example. Instead of manually creating a Sale Items collection, you can mark items as being in the sale category. To do this, add a Merchandise field that uses the choice field type, as shown in Figure 7.20. It fits neatly next to Category if you resize that field.

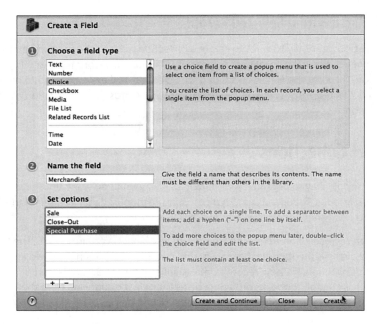

Figure 7.20

Add a merchandise choice field.

Figure 7.21 shows how you can set this field in any record in Inventory.

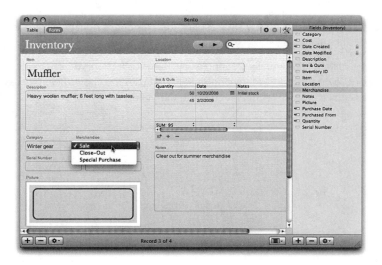

Figure 7.21

Set the field values as necessary.

Now, using either of the techniques described previously, create a query that searches for "sale" in the Merchandise field, as shown in Figure 7.22.

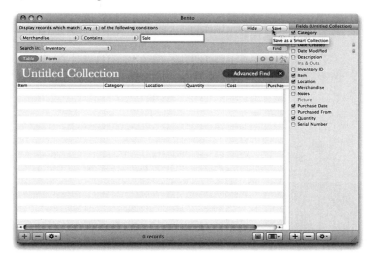

Figure 7.22
Create the Smart Collection.

Click Save to create the Smart Collection. You can rename it something meaningful such as Smart Sale. Now, move through the library and change the Merchandise field on various records to Sale or to other categories. Whenever you change the Sale value on a record, it is added to or deleted from the Smart Sale collection as necessary.

NOTE

Any time you can make a process automatic, your Bento database (like any other database) is more stable. Like related records, Smart Collections rely on data entry and data entry alone for creating links or collections; you do not have to remember to do a second step.

8

Using Built-In Bento Libraries for Address Book

IN THIS CHAPTER

- Exploring the Address Book Library   113

- Extending Bento's Address Book Library with New Fields and Forms   116

- Synchronizing Address Book   118

- Using Mac OS X Data Detectors to Update Address Book   124

Exploring the Address Book Library

In the preceding chapters, you saw how to use Bento to create libraries, collections, records, and forms as well as how to search and edit data. In this chapter and the two that follow, you see how to combine Bento and its tools with Address Book and iCal, applications that are built into Mac OS X. Bento's integration with Address Book and iCal is very tight. If you choose, Address Book data is shown in a Bento library, and iCal data is shown in two Bento libraries: iCal Events and iCal Tasks.

To start, you need to choose this integration. Do so using File > Address Book and iCal Setup, as shown in Figure 8.1.

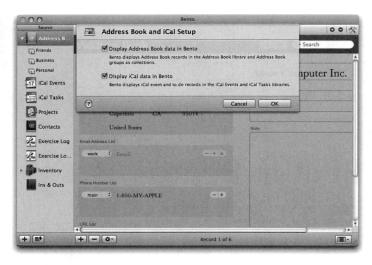

Figure 8.1

Enable Address Book integration.

You now have an Address book library in your Bento source list. Any groups that you have created in Address Book show up in the Bento library as collections in the Address Book library. Figure 8.2 shows a typical Address Book; Figure 8.3 shows that same Address Book in Bento.

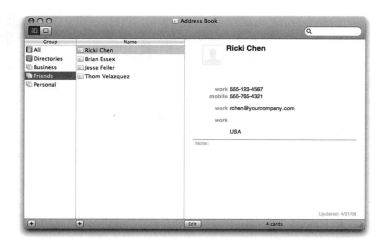

Figure 8.2

Your Address Book data…

Figure 8.3

…can show up in Bento.

You can switch back and forth between Bento and your Address Book to see how the integration works:

- If you add a record in Address Book, it shows up immediately in the Bento Address Book library. If it were added to a group, it shows up in the appropriate Bento Address Book library collection.

- If you add a record in the Bento Address Book library, it shows up in Address Book. If it were added to a collection, it shows up in the appropriate Address Book group.

- If you add a group in Address Book, it shows up in the Bento Address Book library as a collection.

- If you add a collection in the Bento Address Book library, it shows up as a group in Address Book.

Likewise, if you delete a record, collection, or group in one place, it is deleted in the other. There is one area in which the behaviors are not linked. Smart Groups in Address Book are similar to Smart Collections in Bento. As shown in Figure 8.4, you create a Smart Group in Address Book by choosing File > New Smart Group and specifying whatever criteria you want.

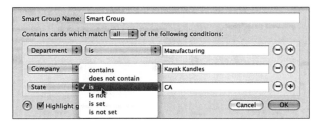

Figure 8.4

Smart Groups in Address Book are, in some ways, like Smart Collections in Bento.

Despite their similarities, Smart Groups in Address Book and Smart Collections in Bento are implemented in different ways, and they are not synchronized between the two applications. If you want, you can easily create a Bento Smart Collection to be the same as an Address Book Smart Group and vice versa.

Extending Bento's Address Book Library with New Fields and Forms

You can add fields to the Bento Address Book library, but before you do so, make certain that the field you want to add does not already exist in Address Book. Many people do not realize that the default template in Address Book shows only some of the available fields. You can use Card > Add Field, as shown in Figure 8.5, to add any of the additional fields that simply are not shown on the template. This command adds the selected field to the given record; if you choose Edit Template, that field is added to the default template.

TIP

If you attempt to enter a duplicate name through Bento, you are warned that the name already exists and you are not able to enter it. If the name you enter is identical except for its capitalization, Bento lets you enter it. Thus, if you accidentally recapitalize an Address Book field name, you are able to create another field. If you rely on the difference in capitalization, you are leaving yourself open to confusion (your own) in the future. Use different names and do not duplicate Address Book data.

Figure 8.5

Add Address Book fields in Address Book.

You can modify Bento forms or create new ones using the Address Book fields. Figure 8.6 shows you the fields available in the Bento Address Book library. They map pretty clearly to the fields in Address Book.

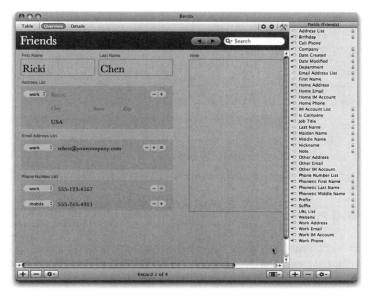

Figure 8.6

Add Address Book fields in the Bento Address Book library.

In Figure 8.7, you can see the fields for the table view of the Bento Address Book library. You can see hierarchies of fields. For example, if you click Home Address, all the fields in that address are added. As Figure 8.7 shows, you can then choose to display only some of those fields.

Figure 8.7

Use field hierarchies in table view.

In both form and table views, some of the fields in the Fields list are locked with a padlock. These fields are in Address Book; you cannot delete them from the Bento Address Book library, although you need not display them on a form or a table.

You can, however, add fields to your Bento Address Book library. These fields can then be displayed on tables or forms in Bento; they do not exist in Address Book, and there is no way to add them there, so they exist only in Bento.

Finally, note how some of the fields, such as phone numbers, use Bento field and interface constructs. There is a phone number list in your Bento Address Book library, and it is the same phone number list that you saw used in Chapter 5, "Working with Phone, URL, IM, and Address Fields and Lists in Contacts."

Synchronizing Address Book

To be precise, Address Book and the Bento Address Book library are not synchronized. *Synchronizing* refers to taking two separate data sources and making their contents consistent. Records may be added to one or the other or deleted from one or the other; changes within records are copied back and forth as necessary until the two data sources are the same.

That does not happen with the Bento Address Book library because, as you have seen, the data resides in Address Book and is displayed and manipulated in the Bento Address Book library even though its storage is in Address Book.

But Address Book itself can be synchronized using a MobileMe account or an iPhone. And as a result of that synchronization, the data that you see in the Bento Address Book library can change.

The common Address Book/Bento fields are synchronized. Fields that you add to the Bento library exist only in that library. They are not synchronized with or shown in Address Book.

NOTE

Most of the time, synchronization just works for you, and you do not have to worry about how it happens. The following sections provide details that you can use to understand the process or to troubleshoot problems.

Synchronizing Address Book with MobileMe

MobileMe is a subscription service from Apple that provides you with a number of features including a me.com address, disk storage on Apple's servers, and synchronization. Apple has long specialized in providing integration to its users—integration of hardware and software, integration among its applications and the operating system, and integration with the Web and through the Web to other computers. For example, with a MobileMe account, you can mount your MobileMe disk storage on your desktop and in Finder windows just by clicking iDisk.

 For more information on MobileMe, go to www.apple.com/mobileme.

When you have a MobileMe account, you set up Address Book synchronization from System Preferences for MobileMe, as shown in Figure 8.8.

Figure 8.8

Set up synchronization with MobileMe.

The settings provided here determine how the data on your computer is synchronized with your MobileMe account. In the lower right, the Advanced button lets you control other computers that are synchronized to the same MobileMe account (see Figure 8.9).

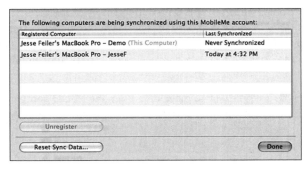

Figure 8.9

Register the computers to be synchronized to a single MobileMe account.

NOTE

You might think that the word "computer" does not need a definition at this point, but, in fact, it does. In the list of computers shown in Figure 8.9, notice that there are two computers with the same name (Jesse Feiler's MacBook Pro). Two separate accounts (Demo and JesseF) are shown. The word "computer" in the world of MobileMe synchronization means a specific user on a specific computer. This means that you can share Address Book and other data among several accounts on the same or different computers. It also means that if you want to synchronize more than one account on a computer with MobileMe, you need to supply the synchronization settings in System Preferences for each of those accounts. And, of course, the reverse situation also applies: if you have two accounts on one or more computers, they can be synchronized to two separate MobileMe accounts.

This synchronization works based on your MobileMe account name. You can have a number of computers registered to your MobileMe account; all of them can be synchronized. The process relies on MobileMe as the center of synchronization. Each computer has its own synchronization settings in its own copy of System Preferences, and each synchronizes with MobileMe according to the schedule that you set. If you do not have an Internet connection, the synchronization cannot happen. Data does not flow directly from Computer A to Computer B without going through MobileMe.

This flow of data matters because it requires at least two separate Internet connections for Computer A to be synchronized with Computer B (A to MobileMe and B to MobileMe). In practice, it often requires three connections (A to MobileMe, B to MobileMe picking up the A changes, and then A to MobileMe picking up changes from B). If you are relying on synchronization to ensure that data is consistent across several computers, remember this sequence.

In practice, unless your Address Book data is changing frequently, as long as each computer connects to MobileMe relatively often (at least once a day for most people), the data will be consistent.

Synchronization usually proceeds just as described here. However, there are cases in which you want to manually synchronize data. The Reset Sync Data button shown at the lower left of Figure 8.9 opens the dialog shown in Figure 8.10. You can choose to replace your local data with the MobileMe data or vice versa. Use the arrows to choose the direction of resetting. Instead of synchronizing, one data set replaces the other. You can do this for all data or specific sets of data from among the checkboxes you have marked in Figure 8.8.

Using this approach can be a simple way to move data from one Mac to another, although if you are installing a new Mac, using a FireWire cable and the Migration Assistant inside Applications > Utilities can be easier.

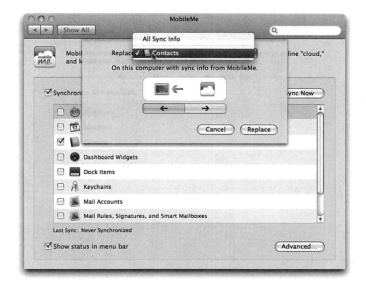

Figure 8.10

Reset Sync Data.

Synchronizing Address Book with iPhone

NOTE

This section describes synchronization using the iPhone connected through a USB port to your computer. The following section describes the new MobileMe push technology in which the iPhone and MobileMe interact directly.

Apple has essentially perfected the synchronization process of music between a computer and an iPod and the further synchronization of music, video, address book, and calendar information between a computer and an iPhone.

As noted previously, the Bento Address Book library does not really synchronize with Address Book because it uses the Address Book data. MobileMe lets you synchronize several computers and/or accounts using the MobileMe server as an intermediary. Synchronization with iPhone is a third architecture: it is direct synchronization without the mediation of MobileMe or the Internet. You plug your iPhone into its cradle and plug the cradle into your USB port. After you have set up your iPhone, iTunes launches and performs the synchronization that you have specified. (You need to set up iTunes for use with your iPhone to be able to activate your iPhone; the instructions are in your getting started package.)

Use iTunes > Preferences to control the backups for your iPhone, as shown in Figure 8.11.

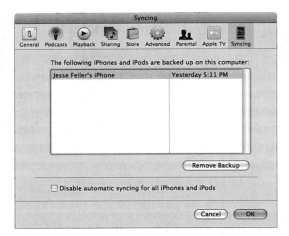

Figure 8.11

Manage synchronization from iTunes Preferences.

In the Info tab of the iPhone window that opens when you plug in your iPhone (or click it in the Devices list at the left), you can control what specific data items are synchronized, as shown in Figure 8.12.

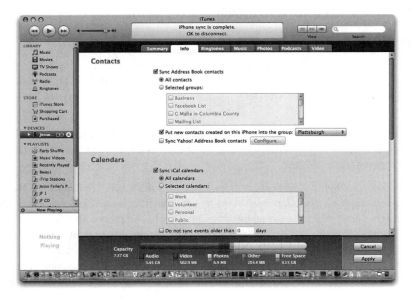

Figure 8.12

Use iTunes to synchronize Address Book and iPhone.

The path from iPhone to your computer and thence to the Bento Address Book library is simple. If you are also using MobileMe synchronization, the path may be more complex, but it usually works without a problem. If your iPhone is paired with another computer or account, the MobileMe synchronization passes that data through to the computer on which your Bento Address Book library is located. Just remember that Bento Address Book is actually displaying and letting you edit the Address Book data on that computer, and that the synchronization with other computers requires MobileMe and Internet connectivity.

If data is not synchronized properly or does not appear where you expect it to, the easiest way to troubleshoot is to take things one step at a time. Because the Bento Address Book/Address Book connection should be the simplest, start there. Then, if you plan to synchronize your iPhone with that computer, connect it and see how the synchronization works. If there are problems, look at the Info tab, as shown in Figure 8.12, to see if you have accidentally opted not to synchronize the relevant data.

Finally, bring the MobileMe synchronization into play. Make certain that you have selected the appropriate synchronization options and that your synchronization schedule is frequent enough to pick up necessary changes.

WARNING

Before starting on synchronization, make certain that you have backed up your hard disk(s) using Time Machine or other backup software. This applies to all the computers that you may be synchronizing with MobileMe. If something goes wrong, you may wind up erasing your contacts. This usually is a result of human error (see the Reset Synchronization Data dialog shown previously in Figure 8.10; if you make the wrong choice, all is lost).

Synchronizing Address Book with PDAs and Other Devices

Other devices that store address book and contact information can often be synchronized with your Mac and thence with MobileMe, other computers, Bento Address Book, and your iPhone. They may connect with a wireless Bluetooth connection or with a cable. Apple makes the Application Programming Interface (API) to iSync and Address Book available to third parties, so they can tightly integrate their products.

The only issues you are likely to encounter have to do with slight inconsistencies in data mapping of multiple phone numbers and addresses. Usually, none of these present insurmountable hurdles.

Do be aware that synchronization is a two-way street. You will often find hardware and software that lets you import data such as address book data. An import is not a two-way transaction; it just lets you move your data from one place to another. And, all too often, after your data has been stored in another device or piece of software, you cannot get it out, and you are tied into that device or software. This problem appears to be somewhat less prevalent than it was a few years ago, but before deciding to use any software that you will use to store your data, make certain that you can get out what you put in.

Using MobileMe Push Technology to Synchronize Data

The replacement of .Mac with MobileMe coincided with the release of the iPhone software version 2.0. For users of iPhone 2, it comes preinstalled. Other users can download it for free using iTunes. Together with MobileMe, this software lets the iPhone synchronize directly with MobileMe rather than with a computer. Your computer, instead, synchronizes with MobileMe over the Internet.

Because the iPhone can handle not just telephony but also Internet data, it can implement the same type of synchronization that a computer uses to synchronize over the Internet with MobileMe: it is just a matter of sending messages back and forth between the iPhone and MobileMe. If you turn Fetch New Data in iPhone Settings to Push, then the iPhone pushes new data to MobileMe as soon as the data is changed on the iPhone: there is no batch synchronization such as the process described previously. Likewise, when changes occur in MobileMe, the relevant changes are pushed down to the iPhone. This means that instead of a possibly lengthy periodic synchronization process, the process is carried out on an as-needed basis, and each process is much shorter because only one item is being synchronized at a time.

An incoming email message to your account on MobileMe is pushed down to your iPhone almost immediately. If you create an appointment on your iPhone, it shows up on your MobileMe account almost immediately. The link between computer and MobileMe, however, does still rely on the synchronization process set up in System Preferences and described in the previous section, so there may be a somewhat longer wait until the data is moved.

Finally, note that the protocols used for all this are basic Internet protocols. That is why you can synchronize Macs as well as PCs with MobileMe.

Using Mac OS X Data Detectors to Update Address Book

Data detectors are interface devices that recognize certain types of data in documents and let you then work with that data in its smart form, not just as a string of text. For example, Figure 8.13 shows a data detector in action in Mail.

As you move the mouse over a data detector, a small dotted line appears around the data that has been identified. A small arrow in the lower right lets you bring up a contextual menu that lets you act on the data that has been detected.

If you choose to update an existing contact, Mail displays the window shown in Figure 8.14. Although the dotted lines surround only the address that was detected, Mail is smart enough to pick up other information from the message so that it can find the contact name. You see the existing data from the contact as well as the updated data that the data detector found in the Mail message. (In the actual window, the updated data is shown in green. In Figure 8.14 that text is slightly lighter than the rest of the text.)

Now the integration of Mac OS X and Bento really shines. If you get in the habit of using the data detectors in your incoming mail, it is just a click of the mouse to add or update your Address Book directly from the Mail message as soon as you receive it. With Bento, iPhone, and MobileMe synchronization in place, that one action updates the information everywhere.

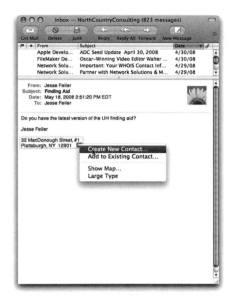

Figure 8.13

Data detectors identify addresses and other data elements.

Figure 8.14

You can create a new contact or update an old one.

The habit of using the data detectors in Mail to update your data immediately is one that pays off not just with contact information but also with iCal information, as you will see in Chapter 9, "Using Built-In Bento Libraries for iCal Tasks and iCal Events." You can easily switch from one application to another in Mac OS X, but by using data detectors and built-in synchronization, you don't even have to do that. You need to take one action (use the data detector), and everything else is done automatically.

Using Built-In Bento Libraries for iCal Tasks and iCal Events

IN THIS CHAPTER

- Catching Up with iCal 127
- Exploring the Bento iCal Libraries 132
- Using Mail's Data Detectors with iCal 134
- Managing Your Calendar Data 135
- Synchronizing iCal Events 137

Catching Up with iCal

In the preceding chapter, you saw how Address Book is integrated with Bento so that data is stored in Address Book but can be displayed or updated either in Address Book or Bento. iCal is integrated with Bento in much the same way, but there are some important differences.

Perhaps the biggest difference is a reflection of the data: iCal data—like all calendaring data—is inherently more complex than address data. People enter, delete, and change calendar data more frequently than address data. Even more important is the time dimension: an event scheduled for yesterday is a different type of information than one scheduled for tomorrow. The one yesterday is, and always will be, in the past. The one tomorrow changes from future to "now" to past as the clock relentlessly ticks. And just to make things more interesting, iCal To Dos may have dates assigned to them, but if the date passes, the To Do is still active until you mark it completed.

NOTE

This chapter focuses on iCal itself. In the next chapter, Chapter 10, "Working with Bento's Projects Library to Use Related Records from iCal Tasks, iCal Events, and Address Book," you see how to bring this functionality deep into your Bento libraries.

As shown in Figure 9.1, iCal displays To Dos in a list at the right of its window. (You can show or hide the To Dos list by using a command from the iCal View menu or by using the pushpin icon at the lower right of all iCal windows.)

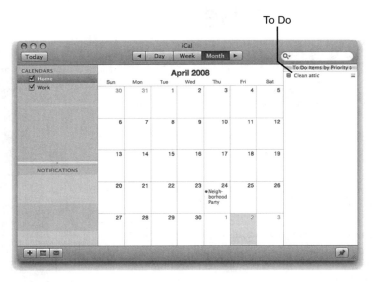

Figure 9.1

iCal To Dos are shown at the right of the window.

At the left of the iCal window is a Calendar list; it too can be shown or hidden with a command from the View menu. iCal events are shown in the center of the iCal window; you can switch this display from days to weeks or months. You also may see the results of a search in a pane that displays search results, as shown in Figure 9.2.

The Search Results pane appears below the calendar and To Do list, but the Calendar list—if shown—is not covered by the Search Results. One reason for this is that, at the bottom of the Calendar list, you can choose to display notifications for events or a Mini Month display, as shown in Figure 9.3.

Search term

Search result

Figure 9.2

Search events and To Dos.

Mini Month display

Figure 9.3

View a Mini Month display below the Calendars list.

Searching for data in iCal reveals part of the underlying complexity. When you type a search word or phrase in the search field at the upper right of the window, iCal searches for that word or phrase in To Dos as well as in events. Figure 9.3 shows both a To Do and an event with the word "clean" in them.

Although there is an intrinsic difference between events and To Dos, there is still a great deal of commonality, as the search results show. Furthermore, many people are not aware of this, but iCal can convert one to the other. If you have an event on a calendar, you can drag it to another date or time; you can also drag its bottom or top down or up to change the start or end time. But if you drag an event to the To Dos list, instead of moving it, you copy it and automatically create a To Do based on the event. The start and stop times don't exist for a To Do, but the date of the event is preserved. Likewise, you can drag a To Do to the calendar; it is copied and an event based on the To Do is created on the calendar.

The *calendars* that can organize events and To Dos are an important part of iCal. iCal begins with Home and Work calendars; you can add more if you want by clicking the plus below the Calendars list. After you have created a To Do (either just now or some time in the past), double-clicking it opens the edit window shown in Figure 9.4. You can then select the calendar you want the To Do to be associated with.

Figure 9.4

Edit a To Do.

The checkboxes next to the calendars in the Calendars list determine which events and To Dos are shown.

NOTE

Calendars enable you to group events and To Dos together. They are somewhat like groups in Address Book. But there is a big distinction: a single address can be in any number of groups (including Smart Groups). An event or To Do can be in only a single calendar. One of the features of Bento's iCal libraries is the capability to organize events and To Dos so that they are in multiple Bento locations.

Because events are inherently more complex than To Dos, double-clicking an event initially opens a summary of its data, as shown in Figure 9.5.

Figure 9.5

Display event details.

If you click Edit, you can then edit the event, as shown in Figure 9.6.

Figure 9.6

Edit an event.

THE ICAL DATA STRUCTURE

iCal is built on the industry standard for Internet calendaring and scheduling ("iCalendar")—RFC 2445 from the Network Working Group of the Internet Engineering Task Force (http://tools.ietf.org/html/rfc2445). The standard was developed to allow the simple sharing of scheduling information using email and the Web. Because this standard is open, it is supported by many products, including iCal. These products store data in whatever format they choose, but they are able to import or export that data in the common format. When such data is sent as an email attachment or embedded in a Web page, the file extension is usually `.ics` and the Web data type is text/calendar.

You, therefore, can use email to share iCal items or to receive them. If you make online reservations for travel or other events, you often have the option to have the reservation data sent to you. More often than not, it is sent as an `.ics` file; when Mail receives the file, by default it opens iCal and inserts the data there. The sender does not have to use iCal or even Mac OS X.

The standard has four main data types: events, To Dos, journals, and free time. Journal data is data associated with a date such as comments or ruminations—a journal just as in the noncomputer world. Free time is just that—time that is not taken up by an event. Currently, not many applications use the journal data. Free time is used in scheduling software. In fact, iCal supports the capability to create events and to invite people via email. It also manages incoming invitations and can automatically create events from them. The Bento libraries support only events and To Dos.

Exploring the Bento iCal Libraries

As you have seen, events and To Dos are related but different in their interface elements and data. Bento handles this issue by providing you with two built-in libraries: one for iCal events and the other for iCal To Dos. If you allow iCal integration using File > Address Book and iCal Integration, as described in the preceding chapter, iCal Events and iCal Tasks are added to your Source list. The data from iCal is displayed in those libraries and stored in iCal.

NOTE

iCal To Dos are Bento tasks. The only difference is the name.

For example, the Neighborhood Party event shown previously in Figure 9.5 is shown in the Bento iCal Events library in Figure 9.7. You can edit the data in Bento, and the changes are immediately shown in iCal itself.

One behind-the-scenes action takes place when you begin to edit iCal data in a Bento library: A new calendar is automatically added to iCal. iCal uses this new calendar, named Bento, for events and tasks that are created by Bento. You can, however, specify another calendar by changing the Calendar field in the Bento library, as shown in Figure 9.7.

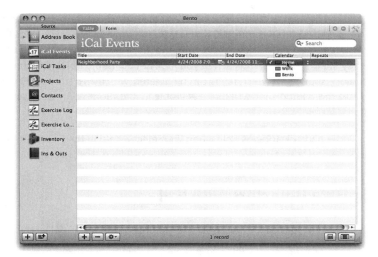

Figure 9.7
Use iCal event data in Bento's iCal Events library.

As you would expect, all the Bento interface tools such as date and time entry are available for editing your iCal data. Figure 9.8 shows the tool you use to edit an iCal event time in Bento. It is the same element you use for editing any date field that includes a time. Note the standard Bento date/time icon in the Start Date and End Date fields in the selected row. The data itself is shown in a row of table view that is not selected, but the selected row is ready for editing with those icons displayed.

Figure 9.8
Use Bento to edit iCal dates and times.

In the Fields list, you see that some of the fields have a padlock next to them. These are the iCal fields; they are stored in iCal and updated through iCal or Bento. You can remove these fields from a given table view or form, but you cannot remove them from the iCal database. You can add new fields in Bento; however, they are not stored in iCal. When you look at your Bento library, the presence or absence of the padlock shows you which fields can be deleted, which also shows you where the data is actually stored and, more important, whether it is visible in iCal. (Bento-only data is not visible in iCal, but everything is visible in Bento.)

New In Bento 2, the padlock appears only when you select a field in the Fields list. If no field is selected, no padlock is shown until you select a locked field that is actually stored in iCal.

Using Mail's Data Detectors with iCal

Mail's data detectors work just as well with iCal as with Address Book.

For information on using data detectors with Address Book, see "Using Mac OS X Data Detectors to Update Address Book" in Chapter 8, "Using Built-In Bento Libraries for Address Book," p. 124.

As shown in Figure 9.9, hovering your mouse pointer over a potential date brings up a dotted line and arrow. If you click the arrow, Mail can decode it so that you can view it in iCal or create a new event. Mail, together with iCal, recognizes dates such as 4/24 and assumes the current year. For a day of the week, it assumes the next occurrence—Monday means next Monday, not last Monday. And "today" means today.

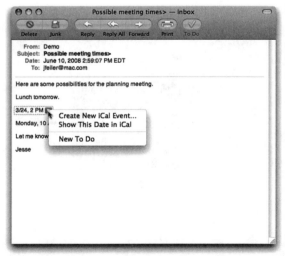

Figure 9.9
Create events directly from Mail.

TIP

If you highlight part of the email message before using the data detector, the highlighted text appears in the Notes field of the event. This capability is useful for a wide variety of data, ranging from reservation confirmation numbers to agendas for meetings that are shown in the email message.

Many people seem to live on email today. For anyone who has played telephone tag trying to schedule something, the asynchronous messaging of email is a welcome relief. You can use data detectors to quickly show a date (and time) in iCal so that you can easily see if a proposed date is free.

The integration with iCal and Address Book means that you can frequently read an email message and handle it then and there; you don't have to remember to put it in your calendar or date book later in a second step. Not only can it save time, but also creating the iCal appointment immediately, means that you don't have partially scheduled appointments floating in limbo around email messages rather than being stored in iCal.

TIP

Over the years, Apple has developed an enormous amount of software and worked on many user interface designs. Not all the development efforts have seen the light of day. Some of them that did see the light of day did not catch on. Apple has worked on the general concept of data detectors for some time. In fact, the Newton handheld device implemented some of this technology.

The Newton's implementation went a step further so that "lunch" or "dinner" could be mapped automatically to a specific time. Apple shipped that code on the Newton, and perhaps it will reappear in the Mail/iCal link. Long-time Apple watchers know that one of the best ways of seeing what Apple will be releasing in the future is to watch for places where technology from past projects can be reused.

Managing Your Calendar Data

In Chapter 10, you see how to use Bento to bring relevant data into Bento libraries. You may be chomping at the bit to get started, but to get the most out of iCal and Bento, take a moment to think about your calendar data and how you manage it.

Managing a calendar is a personal matter. There is no right way or wrong way to do it as long as you show up on time and manage to more or less accomplish the tasks you have to perform. Although there is no right or wrong way to manage your calendar, the fact is that there are two things that can make it more likely you will miss appointments and forget about tasks. Fortunately, iCal and Bento together can address both of these issues if you do your part:

- The first way in which you can make a mess of your calendar is to try to do too much. There are only 24 hours in a day, and if you schedule 30 hours, you won't get everything done. Even if you do not account for too many hours, if you schedule two appointments at the same time, you are in trouble. For many people, the problem arises with the tasks, not with their appointments. An appointment that is in the past is over and done with whether you attended. But a To Do item just sits there and rolls over to the next day until it is done. If you are behind in those tasks, you can easily accumulate quite a handful of undone tasks that together account for perhaps a week's work.

■ The second common way to make a mess of your calendar is to have too many calendars. Not too many in the sense of iCal calendars, but too many in the sense of iCal and other programs, wall calendars, PDA calendars, calendars on shared websites, traditional paper calendars. That makes it remarkably easy to schedule conflicts. In addition, if you have two hours' worth of tasks for today on one calendar, another two hours' worth of tasks on another, before long you may find yourself with more than a day's worth of tasks.

The more you rely on a single calendar to organize your life, the less likely you are to run into the problems described here. iCal lets you share data with other people by publishing calendars to the Web. In addition, if you use iCal invitations, your friends and colleagues can automatically update their calendaring software with the events that you schedule, and, presumably, they will send you invitations that iCal can manage as its own events.

Accumulating multiple calendars is remarkably easy. You may have a schedule for a sports league and a separate schedule for campground reservations. Many organizations rely on free calendaring software on their websites. This proliferation of calendars means that you have to remember to check all of them to find out when you are free or busy.

The best solution is to have a single calendar—iCal. The second-best solution is to move appointments from other calendars into iCal as soon as you find out about them. If someone has a Web-based calendar that you need to refer to, make certain that you can export events from it in `.ics` format. Because this is an open standard, you are asking for the export capability to be available to anyone with modern calendaring software—scarcely an unreasonable request.

TIP

There is one exception to the single-calendar suggestion. If you have a block of time that is scheduled by other people (think of your job, for example), your calendar can just account for the time as a whole. Your work appointments can live separately in their own calendar, which may even be part of a corporate database. The more your work and personal calendars are integrated (flex-time, perhaps, or colleagues from work who are also personal friends), the more you should consider having only one scheduling tool.

The issue of accumulating incomplete tasks is one that you have to address head-on. Make it a point to look at your calendar regularly (once a day for many people) and adjust your incomplete tasks. Do not just roll them over to tomorrow; instead, realistically distribute them in a reasonable schedule until they are done. And if some of them are not going to be done, face the music and delete them. Or delegate them, if that is a possibility. But be realistic. No matter how good you have been, the chance of your dog cleaning out the attic is probably about the same as the chance of your doing it if you have not done it so far. Be creative: move.

This regular review of your schedule is actually more important when you use Bento. As you will see in the following chapter, you can integrate iCal events and tasks with project management in Bento. You can lay out events and tasks for each project in its own context and then view them on an iCal calendar. The project-based scheduling lets you look at things from that project's viewpoint, but you may wind up with an unbalanced schedule. Fortunately, if you overbook a day while updating projects, you can go into iCal, quickly see the conflicts (as shown in Figure 9.10), and change them there. The Bento data reflects the iCal data, so you have to make the change only once. (This technique works for events, but iCal cannot show if you have too many tasks on a given day.)

Figure 9.10
iCal makes it easy to spot scheduling conflicts.

Synchronizing iCal Events

The same process that is used to synchronize Address Book and other data can be used to synchronize iCal events. This is not just a matter of copying data from one place to another. From the standpoint of Bento, this is the process by which your personal information in Bento libraries on your own Mac moves out into the world of other devices. If you are using MobileMe, that information goes into the MobileMe cloud where it can be pushed or pulled to your iPhone, to PCs and Macs, and to any other device registered to your MobileMe account. Those devices, in turn, may also pass the information along to devices with which they synchronize. And, of course, the reverse is true: MobileMe, through its synchronization, brings information from the outside world—other Macs you own, PCs running Outlook, PDAs, and more to your iCal events.

Apple's MobileMe service is the successor to .Mac. It can synchronize iCal events just as easily as Address Book (and more). See Chapter 8, p. 124.

For information about how to add references to your iCal events to your Bento libraries, see Chapter 10, p. 148.

10

Working with Bento's Projects Library to Use Related Records from iCal Tasks, iCal Events, and Address Book

IN THIS CHAPTER

- Exploring Projects 139

- Working with Related Records from iCal and Address Book 142

- Working with Related Records from Mail 146

- Customizing Fields and Revising Forms 148

- Creating and Sharing Calendar Events and Address Book Contacts with MobileMe 148

Exploring Projects

Bento's built-in Projects library integrates Address Book, iCal Tasks and Events, and Bento itself to provide you with a way of managing projects. The integration of the other libraries gives you a powerful way of using the data that you already have. The overall structure of the Projects library provides a way for you to keep track of the projects with which you are involved.

As you move into the second half of this book, you'll find repeatedly that the challenges in setting up Bento libraries do not have much to do with technology: Bento has got that down cold, making databases easier than ever before for you to use. The challenges that you'll find are almost existential: how do you want to organize your life and your data? You will find suggestions from Bento and in the later chapters of this book, but ultimately you will have to decide how you want to do things.

Remember that Bento is not a shared database, so in most cases, it is not the right tool for managing a multiperson project in which everyone is updating his or her own data. The Projects library is an excellent tool for managing a project that you are solely responsible for: you update the data as the project progresses. A shared database with which the members of the project can individually update their own tasks and view the consolidated project information is a task for a more complex database such as FileMaker Pro. This is not a limitation of Bento; it is just an understanding of what Bento's goals are. There are many, many projects in which a single leader is responsible for keeping things moving. For those projects, the Bento Projects library may be just what you want. And remember, too, that the integration with Address Book and iCal means that from your command center in the Bento Projects library, you can easily coordinate events and tasks with your colleagues.

⟳   In Chapter 11, "Designing a Projects Library with Related Notes," p. 157, you see how to expand the Projects library with a record of what has happened along the way.

When you first create a library from the Projects template, you see the window shown in Figure 10.1. Note that this is the Projects template from Bento 1. If you have created a library based on the Bento 1 Projects library, it will appear like this even in Bento 2. The Bento 2 version of the Projects library is discussed later in this chapter.

Figure 10.1

Create a Projects library from the template.

Several aspects of this library are different from the ones you have seen before. First, notice that two forms are provided: Overview and Details. Next, look at the bottom center of the window. There you can see that, instead of one sample record as in the other templates you have seen so far, there are three so that you can get more of a sense of the template's possibilities.

In the Overview form, the Team Members field at the right is a list of related records. The highlighted icon lets you add records from the related table. In this case, as you see in the next section, it is your Address Book.

Explore the Details layout shown in Figure 10.2. Flip back and forth between the layouts to see some good Bento design techniques.

Figure 10.2

The Details form provides greater detail.

Both forms contain the basic information about the project. Overview has fewer details, but it adds the description. Note that both forms leave the basic information about the project in the same location (although the Notes field is smaller in the Overview). If you design a series of forms based on the same database, decide what items you want to preserve on all the forms and then place them in the same location. You may choose to vary this information so that certain items appear on all forms and other items appear only on some forms. But to the extent that you can place the same item in the same place on each form, you will find it easier to work with the forms.

In Bento 2, the Projects library template has been revised to incorporate a significant new feature of Bento 2: direct integration with Mail. Figure 10.3 shows the Bento 2 Projects library Overview form. In addition to team members, you can add email messages to it. This is described later in this chapter in the section "Working with Related Records from Mail."

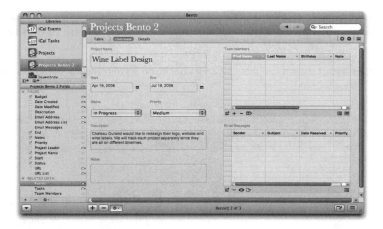

Figure 10.3

In Bento 2, the Projects library template incorporates email messages.

Working with Related Records from iCal and Address Book

The Details form shows the related records from Address Book (Team Members), as well as iCal Tasks and Events.

To add data from a list of related records, click the icon at the lower left of a related records field. (It is highlighted in Figure 10.1.) You then see a dialog that lets you select the record(s) you want to use (see Figure 10.4). You can double-click or Shift-click to select several records. You can also use the search field at the bottom of the dialog to search for records. After you've selected the records you want, click the Add To List button.

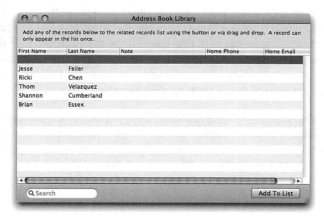

Figure 10.4

Search for records to relate.

TIP

A record can appear in a related records list only once. If you search for records in the related database and the Add To List button is not active, the reason is that the record has already been added. If you select several records, one or more of which have already been added to the related records list, clicking the Add To List button adds the new one and ignores the duplicates.

In Bento 1, when you click on related records list field, the Fields list at the right of the window changes to the fields in the related records database, as shown in Figure 10.5. You can use the checkboxes to determine which fields are shown in the list of related records in Bento.

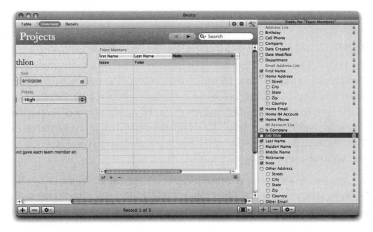

Figure 10.5

Select the fields in related records to be shown in Bento 1.

In Bento 2, the small icon at the lower right of the related records list field has the same effect.

The fields you select to be shown in the related records are shown in the search dialog, as shown in Figure 10.4. However, as Figure 10.6 demonstrates, you can search on any field that exists in the related database. In this case, the string "Platts" is used to search for Plattsburgh—a city name. That field is not shown in the related records list, but you can still search it. This capability is useful for extracting records based on a criterion that matters in the context of Address Book, but not in Bento.

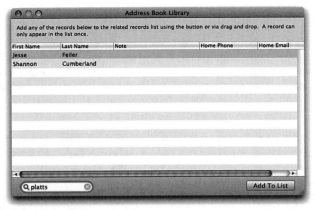

Figure 10.6

Search based on any field.

An example is using an iCal calendar that identifies the project. If you have such a calendar, you can search on its contents to find all records in iCal for calendar Project X, for example. You can then select them all and add them to the list of related records in Bento with a single click. But there is no point in showing the calendar name in your Bento list of related records; it is the same for every record in your list (Project X). Because Bento searches in all fields, you can search on Project X, select the records, and then continue on your way.

After you have established the link, the affected records are shown in the list of related records in Bento at all times. Remember that this is not a Smart Collection: if the search criterion is no longer valid, the record remains in the list of related records until you manually remove it. As is the case with all related records, if you create a new record in the list, it is stored in Address Book and related back to your Bento database.

For example, you can type into the Team Members related records list in the Projects library to add a new team member, as shown in Figure 10.7.

When you go to Address Book, that person is now included in the Address Book without doing anything else, as shown in Figure 10.8. Furthermore, if you type a note into the Address Book record, it immediately appears in the Notes column of the Team Members field in Projects.

If you are filling a project with data from iCal and Address Book, you will probably use the searching technique frequently. On the other hand, if you are starting a new project from scratch, you may do your data entry in Bento and rely on its being updated externally. Of course, you may choose both: your project members may already be in your Address Book, but the tasks you create may be more logically created in Bento.

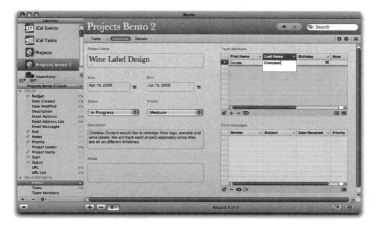

Figure 10.7

Add a new team member in the related records list in the Projects library.

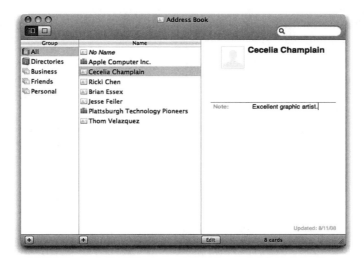

Figure 10.8

Data is automatically shared from Address Book to Projects.

Although Bento can make your life much easier with this integration, there is one point you should bear in mind: the data you enter either in Bento, in Address Book, or iCal is shown in the other application, and it is often shown in a different context. Figure 10.9 illustrates an example in which this can cause a problem.

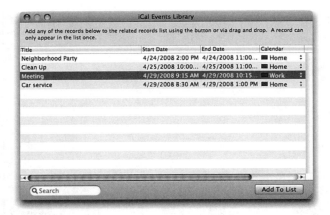

Figure 10.9

Avoid ambiguous event and task names.

If you were importing data into a Bento project, would you choose to import an event labeled simply as "Meeting"? What meeting? You can use iCal calendars to organize your data there, and you can see the calendar data in Bento, but that may not be enough.

Here are some of the ways you can prevent confusion. Use any or all of them (or others) that make sense to you. Remember that confusion can go in both directions. If you add an event called "Meeting" to the related records list for a project, it is very clear what that event is as long as you are in Bento. When you look at that event in iCal, it is a big mystery.

- Create an iCal calendar for each of your Bento projects and assign the appropriate tasks to it. Then you can use the Bento search to quickly find new records to be added. Do this whenever you think there might be new ones. As noted previously, Bento makes certain that you do not add related records twice.

- If there is likely to be any ambiguity, use an abbreviation for the project in the name, such as "ABCProj: meeting." Just make certain you use the same abbreviation everywhere else. (You can also place this in the notes or other field for the item.)

- Make certain the event name is unambiguous. This means clearly identifying the project, and it involves more typing than the two preceding methods.

Working with Related Records from Mail

One of the significant new features of Bento 2 is integration with Mail. Mail integration is slightly different in its interface from the iCal and Address Book interfaces. There, and in other related records list fields, you can search for data to add to the related records list, as shown in Figure 10.10. In a related list of email messages, that icon opens Mail itself. You use Mail's searching and organizing tools to select the messages you want to relate.

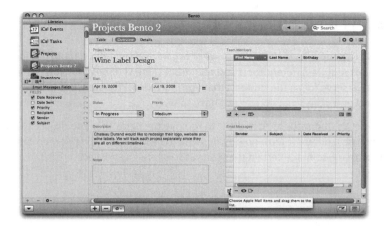

Figure 10.10

View email messages to Bento.

As Figure 10.11 shows, you can choose email messages or other messages such as RSS feed messages from Mail. When you click the Choose Apple Mail Items icon shown in Figure 10.10, Mail opens so that you can select and drag the messages you want into Bento field. Any type of Mail message can be used in Bento: if it is in Mail, you can add it to a Bento email message list.

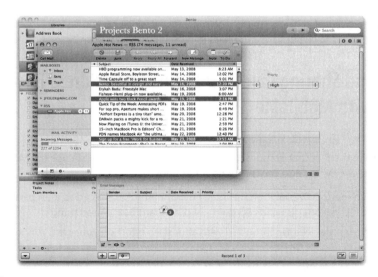

Figure 10.11

Add email messages to Bento.

Customizing Fields and Revising Forms

As noted previously, people have their own ways of organizing calendar data. In addition, different projects sometimes require different tools and techniques. The changes that you make in the Projects library itself have to serve for all the projects that you will use. Fortunately, Bento is so easy to modify (and remodify and unmodify) that you do not have to worry.

One of the simplest customizations to make is to remove the fields that you do not need from the forms. Also, if you use a different terminology, feel free to rename the fields. Remember that Bento is your personal database, so make certain that your user—you—is satisfied.

> **NOTE**
>
> Initially, remove the fields from the forms, not from the database. Then, when you are satisfied that you really do not need them, you can remove them from the database. Remember that once a field is removed from the database, its data is gone. Cleaning up is good, but wait to do your cleaning until you are satisfied with your changes.

Add and Revise Forms

As you work with the Projects library, you may find that you want different ways of looking at the data. Remember that you can not only modify forms but also create new ones. Make the data as clear as you can. Often that means creating extra forms to display the project data in different ways. If you have two or three types of projects (such as projects you work on by yourself, volunteer projects, and projects at work), you may want to see the data in different ways for each type of project.

Creating and Sharing Calendar Events and Address Book Contacts with MobileMe

iCal and Address Book both can synchronize with other computers, iPhones and other devices, and MobileMe. Despite the fact that Bento is designed for a single user, you can use the MobileMe synchronization to share events and contacts with other people.

MobileMe is much more powerful than the .Mac environment that preceded it (in part because of advances in Web technology). It winds up doing two different but related things:

- It keeps all your devices synchronized with almost no effort on your part; your data is the same on all of them.

- It allows you to synchronize some or all of your data with other people on Macs or PCs. In this way, it is a bridge from the private world of your Mac (or Macs) and your iPhone or PDA to other people.

The first step is to create a MobileMe account if you do not have one. To do so, go to http://www.mobileme.com.

When you have the account, the next step is to set up your initial synchronization preferences. MobileMe stores its data on the Internet, in what is called a *cloud*. You can access it from anywhere that you have an Internet connection. The basic setup of your MobileMe data is shown in Figure 10.12.

Figure 10.12
Set up your initial MobileMe settings.

If you want to synchronize your data with another Mac of yours (perhaps home or office), the setup for that Mac is basically the same. In fact, synchronizing with a PC running Outlook on Windows XP or Vista is the same basic process.

The integration that MobileMe makes possible is important, but Bento takes it even further. Figure 10.13 shows an Address Book record viewed in the web interface to MobileMe (www.me.com). It is similar to the Address Book interface that you have on your desktop. Compare Figure 10.13 to Figure 10.9. Not only do you see the similarities, but also if you have followed the sequence of steps in this chapter, you realize that entering a new team member in the related records list for a project in Bento updated Address Book and, through MobileMe, the Address Book data on the Web. Furthermore, although you don't see it, that data has now been updated on your iPhone and perhaps other computers.

Figure 10.13

A contact entered in Bento flows through Address Book to MobileMe and then to other devices.

Whether it is a contact, an event, or a task, most people think about entering the data when they are working with it—for example, when they are working on the particular project that contact, event, or task is associated with. In the bad old days (before Bento), you had to switch from what you really wanted to do (manage the project) to update your address book or calendar. Now, all that maintenance is done for you automatically through Bento, MobileMe, and the Mac OS X applications.

CAUTION

There is one thing to watch out for. If you add a contact, event, or task through a Bento-related records list, the appropriate data source (Address Book or iCal) is updated with the new record. If the contact, event, or task already exists, you wind up with duplicate entries. In most cases, this is not a major problem because you probably know, in general, who is in your Address Book and what is likely to be in iCal. For example, if you add someone you know to a Bento project, that person is likely to be in your Address Book. If it is someone new and you are copying information from a business card you have just been given, chances are the person is not in your Address Book. If there is any possibility, search for the person, task, or event as described previously in this chapter.

11

Designing a Projects Library with Related Notes

IN THIS CHAPTER

- Exploring the Projects Library 151

- Organizing and Implementing Notes: The Basics 154

- Enhancing the Relationship 161

Exploring the Projects Library

For many people, the first step in developing your own Bento library is to find a Bento library template that comes close to what you want. Then, create a library from the template and start to explore it. As you do, you may realize that you want to make changes.

This chapter provides a walk-through of one such customization. When you are dealing with something such as projects, the way you work determines what you need Bento to do. The basic Projects template lets you describe the project, add notes, and associate information from Address Book (team members) and iCal (tasks and events). In Bento 2, you can also add messages from Mail. The Bento 1 version of Projects is shown in Figure 11.1 with the Overview form selected.

Figure 11.1

The Bento 1 Projects library template combines information in the Overview form.

In Bento 2, the Projects template has been expanded to include Mail, as shown in Figure 11.2.

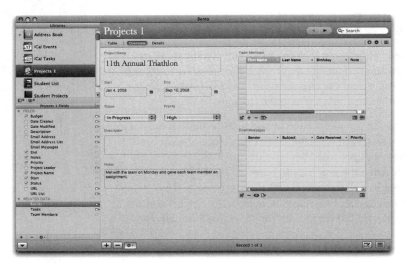

Figure 11.2

The Bento 2 Projects library includes email messages.

Whether you are using the Bento 1 or Bento 2 version of the template, you can rearrange things as you see fit. Perhaps you tend to work with larger or smaller teams: You can change the size of the Team Members related list field to reflect that.

As you can see in the previous figures, a Notes field is included in the library. As you start to explore the library, you may discover what may be a limitation for you.

The sample data in Figure 11.3 shows the project lasting over a period of eight months. The note says, "Met with the team on Monday and gave each team member an assignment." Which Monday? How many such notes might accumulate in this Notes field over the course of the project? How will you find the new ones, let alone deal with old ones?

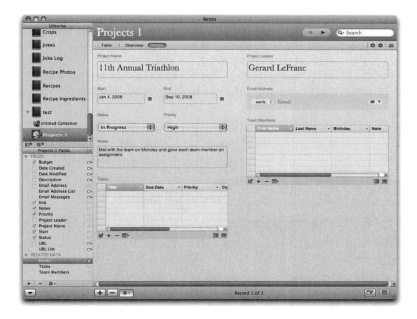

Figure 11.3

The Bento 2 Projects template Details form adds information to the Overview form.

iCal manages tasks and events—things that happen in the future. You can look at events from the past as well as completed tasks, but the emphasis in any calendar is on the future.

One aspect of project management for many people is keeping track of what has happened in the past—items such as the sample note in Figure 11.1. Because iCal and the Bento Projects library handle tasks and events, if you want to organize and structure your notes, you have to do so yourself. In this chapter, you see how to construct a table for notes that you can relate to a modified version of the Projects library.

Organizing and Implementing Notes: The Basics

The whole point of using a database is to organize your data so that you can easily retrieve it as you need it. Bento makes it easy not only to structure the data but also to modify the structure as well as the data. One way to go about creating a Notes table to be related to Projects is simply to create a table with a single field—Note—and relate it. This section shows you how to do that. You can then modify the Notes table to add additional fields and to structure it a bit more. The following section shows you how to do that.

> **NOTE**
>
> For most people, creating a Bento library is an iterative process. Remember: you are the user. You can do what you want. In general, it is a good idea not to remove fields from the database unless you are certain that the data they contain appears elsewhere or doesn't matter. (It is easy to forget that a field not required for the current record in a database may matter very much for other records.) If you find yourself modifying your libraries and database a great deal, consider the tips later in this chapter in the section "Enhancing the Relationship."

Remember that by implementing notes as a related table, you are able to use all the relational tools that Bento supports, including the display of records in a scrolling list, the summary row at the bottom, and the like.

The steps involved in creating the related table are

- Create a new Bento library for notes and call it Project Notes.
- Create the basic fields in Project Notes.
- Add a list of related records to the Projects library.

Each of these steps is detailed in the following sections.

Create a New Bento Library for Notes

The first step in creating a related table is to create a new library. Choose File > New Library or click the Add Library (plus) button below the Source/Libraries list. Instead of selecting a built-in Bento library, choose the Blank library and name it Project Notes, as shown in Figure 11.4.

> **NOTE**
>
> There is a built-in Notes library template. Naming this library Project notes keeps it separate.

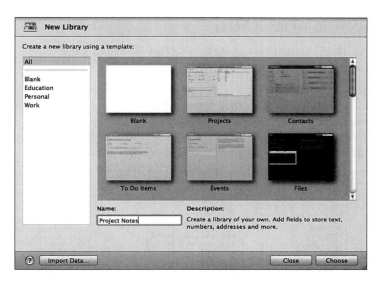

Figure 11.4

Create a Notes library.

The two default fields, Date Created and Date Modified, are in the new library as always, although they are not added to the basic form, as shown in Figure 11.5.

Figure 11.5

The new library has the two default fields.

In addition to the default fields, you need a field to store the note.

Create the Basic Field in Project Notes

The next step is to create a Notes field. Choose Insert > New Field or click the Add Field (plus) button below the Fields list.

In the dialog shown in Figure 11.6, it is relatively obvious that this should be a Text field. Should it have the autocomplete option set? That choice is something that you probably need to work out for yourself as you work with the data. (There is more discussion of this issue later in this chapter in "Enhancing the Relationship.") If your notes tend to be repetitive (such as "check on this,") autocomplete can be useful; if they are not, autocomplete can be a nuisance.

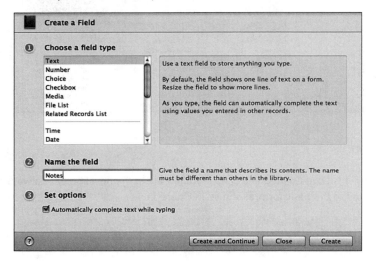

Figure 11.6

Add the Notes field.

If you were building a Bento library to use on its own, at this point you would probably start working on one or more forms for your interface. However, in this case, the Project Notes library at this point is going to be used only for related records in the expanded Projects library, so you can move on.

NOTE

With Bento, you can always come back to make changes. Very few actions in Bento are not reversible (except for the deletion of fields and libraries themselves).

Add a List of Related Records to the Projects Library

You now have a library that can hold related records. All you have to do is add a related records list. The simplest way is to select a form in the Projects library and drag the Project Notes library from the Source/Libraries list onto that form. As you drag it, you see the outline of the related records list field. Behind it, you see the form rearranging itself to accommodate the new field. Figure 11.7 shows what it looks like in the middle of the drag-and-drop process before you have released the mouse button.

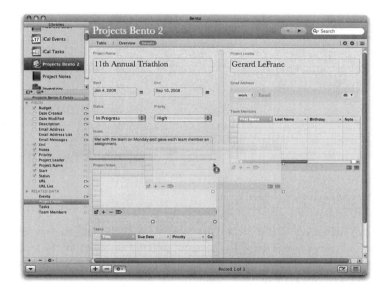

Figure 11.7

Create a related records list in the Projects library.

When you release the mouse button, the new related records list field is created in the form, and the field itself shows up in the Fields list, as shown in Figure 11.8. In Bento 2, the Projects Notes library shows up in the Related Data section at the bottom of the Fields list, which is also shown in Figure 11.8; in Bento 1, it shows up as a field that is alphabetized in the Fields list among the local fields. Wherever it is, if you want to change the name of the related records list field from the default name (the name of the related library) to another name, just double-click the name in the Fields list and change the name.

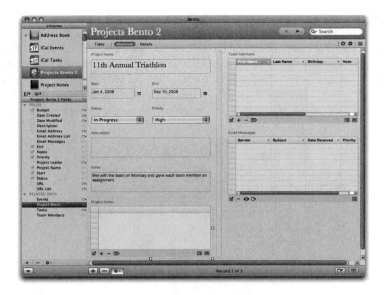

Figure 11.8

Add the Project Notes library as a related records list field.

By default, the fields shown in a related records list field are the fields that you have selected to be shown in the related library's table view. If you have not selected any fields for the table view, none show up in the related records list field. In that case or in any other in which you want to add fields to the related records list view, do one of the following:

- In Bento 1, click the related records list field. The Fields list changes to show the fields in the related library. Click the checkboxes of the field(s) you want to add to the related records list field into that field and rearrange them as you see fit.

- In Bento 2, click the icon in the lower right of the related records list field, which changes the Fields list to show the fields in the related library. Click the checkboxes of the field(s) you want to add to the related records list field into that field and rearrange them as you see fit.

To test your changes, copy the single note from the old Notes field and paste it into the first line of the related records list field. Choose the Notes library from the Source/Libraries list so that you can view the data. At this point, you do need a field in the form, so add the Note Text field. As you can see in Figure 11.9, the pasted note text is visible in the Notes library. You now have a way to enter multiple notes.

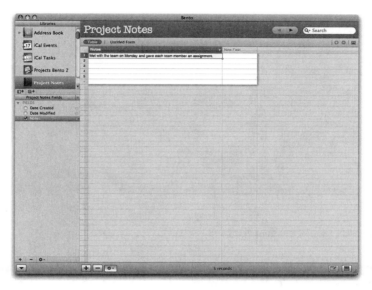

Figure 11.9

The related Notes records are updated automatically from Projects.

One further enhancement is to add the Date Modified field for Project Notes to the related records list in Projects, as shown in Figure 11.10. You can sort on this field to find the most recently modified notes and review them. By using related records, you transform the free-format Notes field in the Projects library template into a structured collection of individual notes. In general, any time you can do such a transformation, handling your data is easier.

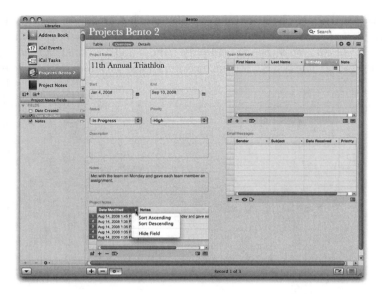

Figure 11.10
Add Date Modified to the related records list field.

If you want, you can add more fields to the Notes library, but with Bento, simplicity is key. Maybe you think that it would be a good idea to add a Completed field to a note to show that it has been handled. But that duplicates tasks for iCal. If something needs to be completed, it is a task, not a note. Many experienced database designers start to think how new features can be added using the existing data structures that they have. If you need a new feature and need to modify the structure, doing so is easy in Bento. But if you can work a variation on the existing structure, that variation simplifies the structure (and also helps you remember where you have put the data!).

CAUTION

Reusing existing structures does not mean putting multiple types of data in a single field. If you need both a note field and a field to store the phase of a project to which it applies, create a project phase field. Once you start cramming unrelated items into single fields, you start to make the database unnecessarily complex. And using special codes or values within a field is a definite no-no. If you are tempted to use a date such as 1/1/2001 to mean "no such data," do not do it. Reusing the structure means getting as much as you can out of the structure you have, but if you need a new field, add it rather than muddying the structure.

Enhancing the Relationship

The Project Notes library that is created here is as generic as can be: you have added only one field to the two default ones. You can use it as related records in almost any library to which notes might apply (which is probably just about any library). Notes can be a record of what you have done, phone calls, or meetings.

In Figure 11.11, you see an additional note added to the Triathlon project.

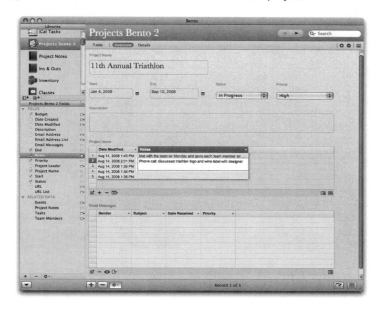

Figure 11.11

Add more notes using the Projects library.

But wait a minute…. The note references a phone call during which you discussed the logo for the triathlon as well as the design of a wine label. It is reasonable that you might discuss two projects when you are talking to one person—particularly as is the case here, when that person is a designer working on both projects.

You could create two notes, one for each project, but the reality of such a conversation often is that it bounces back and forth from one to another. If you create a single note, as shown in Figure 11.11, it is automatically related to the first project (Triathlon, in this case). You can then go to the other project and add the same note to that project, by clicking the icon in the lower left and choosing to add it, as shown in Figure 11.12.

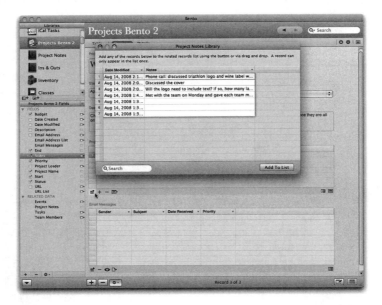

Figure 11.12

Add a note to more than one project.

You can use the arrows at the right of the navigation bar to switch between the two projects: you see that the note is attached to both of them.

But you can do more. You have related the Project Notes library to the Projects library, but the relationship also can work in the other direction. In the Project Notes, drag the Project library icon from the Sources/Libraries list to create a related records list field based on Projects. Figure 11.13 shows the Project Notes library with this related records list added.

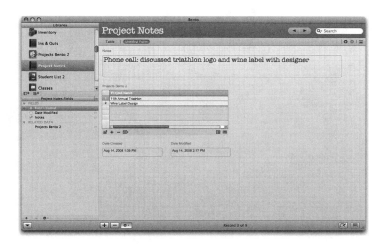

Figure 11.13

The relationship works in both directions.

In Bento 2, an icon in the lower right of a related records list takes you to the selected record in the other library. It opens in the last view (table or form) that you used in browsing that library. In that related record's view, you see a Back button at the right of the navigation bar, as shown in Figure 11.14. The Back button takes you back to the original record. If you have implemented both sides of a relationship as described in this section, you can use the go to related record button in the lower left of a related records list field and the Back button to switch back and forth from one side of the relationship to the other.

Adding notes (or phone calls or conversations) to project records helps to consolidate information in one place. By using related records, you can keep them separate and organized. You can also use Bento's relational capabilities to relate a single record to multiple records in a library, as is the case with a multitopic meeting or phone call.

In addition, you can look at all your Project Notes in table view, sorting them as you want (most likely by date). You can keep track of what you were doing from day to day; as you see each note, you can switch to a form view to look at more details, see the project(s) with which it is associated, and go to the project to get more information.

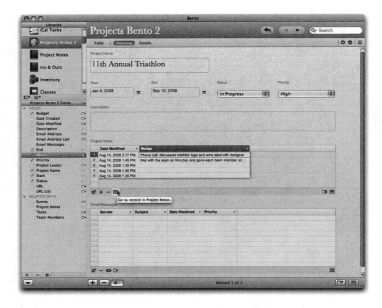

Figure 11.14
Go to related records.

This ability to switch contexts from what you were doing across all projects to a specific project is a powerful part of Bento's relational functionality. It happens with iCal, which also presents your information in a date-ordered sequence while at the same time you can organize events and tasks by Bento project or other library.

In general, keeping your Bento libraries relatively simple and focused and using relationships to join them together can make your solutions powerful and robust. Jumbling everything together starts to work against the idea of organizing information. Before you know it, you have reinvented your center desk drawer.

12

Building a Garden/Nature Log

IN THIS CHAPTER

- Planning the Garden/Nature Log 165

- Creating the Database 167

- Analyzing the Database and Using Smart Collections 173

Planning the Garden/Nature Log

This chapter helps you build a project from scratch. (The Project Notes library in the preceding chapter was designed primarily as a related records repository, so it does not really count as a full-fledged project.) Most of the remaining projects in this book are from-scratch projects like this, although several of them integrate other data sources.

Each project focuses on a specific problem. You have seen the basics of Bento and how it can handle general tasks, but as you move into the particular areas that interest you, you will find that you need to work on the intersection between Bento's power and generalities and the specific needs of the problem you are addressing.

This project is a garden/nature log. (You might also call it a journal or diary.) You can use it to track your garden over the course of a year; you can also use it if you want to keep a nature journal. It stands as a model for any Bento library that you will update on a regular basis with observations of any sort—text, photos, or numeric.

TIP

This project is also very good either for kids or for a family to work on together. You could even use it in a classroom setting, but because Bento is a single-user database, updates have to be done from a central location. These updates could be made by the teacher, a group of students working together, or a rotating roster of students.

Each record is a single observation, just like any Bento record. But you have to decide what that single observation will be. In the case of a log like this, it could be a single day's data; it could also be a summary for a week or month. In planning the project, think about how you will use it and then watch how you actually use it. The most obvious type of observation is daily, but if you garden only on weekends, perhaps your observation should be weekend-by-weekend, not day-by-day.

You also should think about how pedantic you will be about keeping your log. Each observation can be a day's data, but you may choose to enter that data periodically—on the first of the month, once a week, or whenever you have the time. (In many climates, gardeners have the time to keep their garden logs in the winter when nothing is growing. Summertime allows little time for garden logs.)

TIP

As always with Bento, devote a small amount of time to thinking about what you want to do and then jump right in. Use a template as a starting point or create your own library. Use it, and watch how you use it. Your experiences as you use it will help you refine both the Bento library and the ways in which you use it.

Within each record, a variety of observations and measurements could be stored:

- A text description of the conditions such as the weather in general ("afternoon storms"), storms ("visit from Toby and Anni"), special events ("Alisia's birthday"), highlights ("first zucchini" or "groundhog wins the battle for snow peas"), and so forth.
- One or more photos. You can also add videos either as interviews or comments or to show events that highlight movement (wind, deer eating your vegetable garden, and so forth).
- Times of sunrise and sunset.
- Measurements: temperature, precipitation, and possibly wind speed.

With Bento, you can easily modify the database and forms, so you do not have to make a final decision at this point. But there is one point that you should consider. For a database such as this, although it may appear that you are recording data at a given point in time, most of the time you are recording data over a span of time. For example, if you record sunrise and sunset, those are two separate events over a span of time. The span may be a single day, but if you have a routine for updating a diary, you may decide that your "day" starts right after the previous diary entry and continues until the next one. That means you may have more than one sunrise and sunset. It also may mean that if you update the diary daily, the first event would be sunset yesterday, and the second would be sunrise today.

In a similar vein, if you are recording precipitation, it is measured over a period of time, and that period may be a day or it may be a given storm. Thus, you might have two separate rainstorms in one day, and you could record the rainfall from each one separately. Or if you have a storm that lasts several days, you might want to record the total rainfall at the end of the storm.

Bento fills in creation and modification dates, but you probably also need to enter the date of the data. You may skip a day of entering and need to enter two days' worth of data, for example.

TIP

You can use the techniques described in Chapter 11, "Designing a Projects Library with Related Notes," to help organize the data, particularly if your log records cover more than one day. You can create a related table for measurements and relate them to the date range of your primary log record. That lets you record daily temperatures in a weekly or monthly log record. Any single value can be converted to a related value if there may be multiple identifiable instances of that value (by hour or day, for example).

How you structure the database depends on what you are using it for. This chapter shows just one avenue you might explore.

NOTE

A garden journal or nature diary lets you record what you see. There are records from weather services of temperatures, precipitation, and the like. Measurements at your home or where you travel may be different, and you may enjoy making—or need to make—them yourself. You can follow the procedures in Chapter 15, "Importing and Exporting Bento Data and Libraries," to import publicly available data into your Bento database.

Setting up the library and then entering the data is just the first step in creating a garden journal. You can look back on it and see how things grew (or did not grow) over the course of your growing season. In addition, this type of data is very useful for analysis. Later in this chapter, you see how you can use Bento's search features and Smart Collections to track, for example, the first and last frost.

Creating the Database

As you plan the database, you can make a list of the fields that you want to track. At that time, you may realize you need more or fewer fields. Then, as you start to build the database, you also may decide to modify your field list. Whether you plan it in detail or just let it evolve as you work with Bento is up to you.

Creating the Basic Library

Begin by creating a Bento library. You might want to choose the theme for it now. You might use the Starfield theme, for example: it has a green background, so it's a natural fit for the garden theme. Remember that you can always change the theme by selecting another; your layout of fields on a form is unchanged with the new theme. Name the form and you are ready to start creating fields.

You might want to start with a date field. It can be a pair of fields (starting/ending), or it can be a single date or date and time for the observation. Add it with Insert > New Field or with the + icon beneath the Fields list (at the right in Bento 1, and at the left in Bento 2). In the example shown in Figure 12.1, the field is called "24 hours ending"; it is a date field with the option to also display the time. (Such a field is usually referred to as an *as-of date*.) You can add it to the form now by dragging it from the Fields list. The Bento date and time interface elements are automatically provided and are shown when you click the date/time icon in the field.

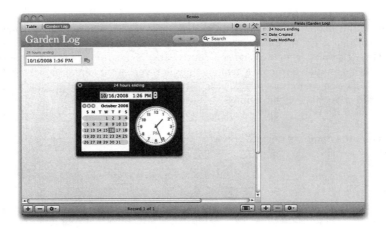

Figure 12.1
Create the first field.

Whether you add all the fields to the database first and then add them to the form does not matter; you can add one or more fields to the database and then add them to the form. That is the method shown in this chapter, but you can use whatever technique works for you.

The next items added to the form are the high and low temperature. Because these fields are logically related fields, they should be near one another. In this example, they are placed at the top of the form, next to the as-of date. This addition automatically enlarges the first column in the default two-column layout of Bento 1, as shown in Figure 12.2.

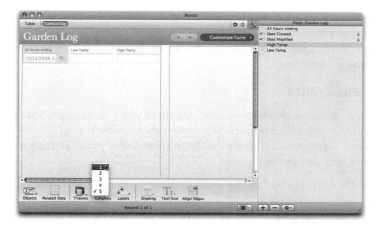

Figure 12.2

Refine the form with fields, themes, and columns.

If you want to add video or a photo, you can add a media field. In this example, it is called Look at This! The naming conventions for fields vary from library to library and person to person. Here, in an informal Bento database, the field names—which appear on the form—are used for descriptive information (such as 24 hours ending) as well as interface tips such as Look at This!

To add to this section, you might want to add a text field called Highlights of the Day. For a field like this, remember not to have autocomplete selected. That option is useful when you are likely to be entering the same data that you have entered previously (a name, perhaps). Finally, you might want to put a rating field into the database so that you can give the day the appropriate number of stars.

After fields have been rearranged and moved around, one possible version of the form is shown in Figure 12.3.

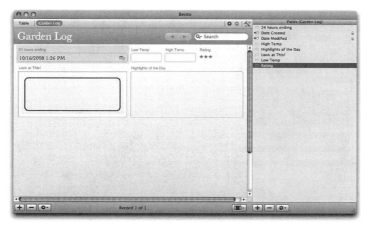

Figure 12.3

Complete the basics.

You can add any of the fields suggested previously in this book. They are all similar to the fields you have used in this example so far. You can also add some related records just as you did with Project Notes in the preceding chapter. The principle here is the same: by organizing free-format data, you make it more usable in searches.

Creating Related Libraries

One candidate for a related records list would be a database that focuses on particular plants and crops. If you want to create related records, create a new database for them; you can call it Crops. This database lets you record information about specific crops and what you have done with them (planted, harvested, fertilized, and so forth).

You need at least the following fields in the Crops database:

- **Crop:** This can be a choice (popup menu). Using a choice means that you will not enter "vinca" in one place and "myrtle" in another. You can always double-click the field in the Fields list and add more choices. In some cases, the crop may be ambiguous; in other cases, for a garden it may be specific such as Spirea (front) or Spirea (back) to indicate two separate bushes.

- **Date:** This is the date on which you did something. It may or may not be the date the record is created, and it may or may not be the date of the Garden Journal record. You can use Insert > Current Date and Time to set this field and then modify it as needed.

- **Activity:** This is what you did. Again, a choice field is a good idea here so that you minimize the number of activities and do not have several names for the same activity.

- **Notes:** This is a free-format field to capture things that do not fit anywhere else.

- **Amount:** You may also want to indicate the amount of what you sowed or harvested (or plowed under).

Figure 12.4 shows what the Crops database might look like if you have created these fields.

Figure 12.4

Create a Crops database.

With a Crops database created, you can now add a related records list to the Garden Journal. This list uses records from the Crops database. Use the techniques described in Chapter 11 to add the related records list. Remember that you can change its name, as shown in Figure 12.5, where the Crops library's related records field is renamed Activities.

Figure 12.5

You can rename a related records list field.

In Figure 12.6, you can see how the completed Garden Log library looks with related records added. You can enter the data for the related records directly from the Garden Log.

Figure 12.6

The Garden Log library is almost finished.

The last step for now is to tidy up the interface for the related records. In Bento 2, you can use the icon at the lower left of the Activities field to go to a selected record in Activities (the Crops library). That record might have a great deal more information about the activity in question. You can view it, update it, and then return to the original Garden Log record. If you have not navigated to another Garden Log record in the meantime, just select the Garden Log library from the Libraries & Fields pane at the left of the window. However, if you want a foolproof way of returning, add the Garden Log library as a related library to the Crops library so that the backwards link is there, as shown in Figure 12.7. (In Bento 2, you can use the Back button to return.)

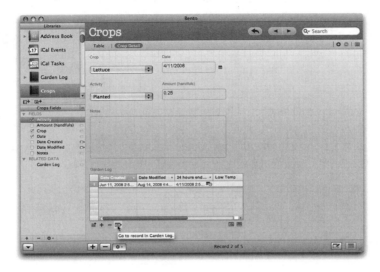

Figure 12.7

Add a backward link from Crops to Garden Log.

With the links in place, you can use the table views for Garden Log and Crops to get a high-level summary (usually by sorting a date field), and then you can move into a form view for a specific day or event (see Figure 12.8). From there, you can always go to a corresponding record in the other library by using the go to related record icon in the lower left of a related records list.

Figure 12.8

Use the table view for fast navigation.

Analyzing the Database and Using Smart Collections

You now have a structure in which to record information. If you are like most gardeners, you like to look back to see how you did in the last growing season. (For gardeners in cold climates, this task is performed in the winter when it begins to seem the snow will never go away.)

The most obvious basic analysis is to use the summary row in the table view to look for minimum and maximum temperatures, as shown in Figure 12.9.

This information is interesting, but for gardeners with winter to contend with, it is not the most crucial information. For gardeners who contend with frost, the critical information consists of the date of the first frost and the date of the last frost: these dates delimit the main growing season.

Figure 12.9

Use the summary row in table view to view minimum and maximum temperatures.

To find these dates, you need to create a Smart Collection that shows all the records with a low temperature below 32 degrees. Click Advanced Find in the Search box and then construct a query to find all records with a low temperature below 32 degrees, as shown in Figure 12.10. After you click Save, remember that you should rename the Smart Collection in the Source list (to something like Frost) so that you will remember what it is.

Figure 12.10

Create a Smart Collection to isolate frost and nonfrost low temperatures.

Having created a Smart Collection, you can then sort it based on the dates. If the records are sorted in ascending order, the first and last frost is immediately evident for a given year. (You can add an additional criterion to the advanced find so that in addition to checking the low temperature, you also look for dates within a given year.)

Bento is particularly useful in this calculation because, at the time that it happens, it is not clear when the last frost occurs. The first frost is simple: it is the first time you have frost for a given year, and you can usually tell it has occurred because tender plants wilt, shrivel, or turn brown. However, the last frost is defined as the frost after which no other frosts occur in that growing season. That means that until all danger of frost is past, you cannot tell when the last frost occurred. With Bento, you can simply look at the table view of the frost Smart Collection, sort it by date, and check for the last frost.

Gardens, nature, and frosts are scarcely the only complex data structure you are likely to deal with. What Bento brings to bear is a way of organizing your data so that you can apply the idiosyncratic rules for each of the issues in which you are interested.

The Crops related records database is useful in its own regard here. You can use the same Smart Collection and search techniques to isolate ranges of dates or specific crops or activities across a variety of Garden Log records. This is the sort of thing that you can do easily when your data is organized in a database. The Garden Log records reflect everything for a specific day, but you can use Crops to look at everything that happens to a specific crop across a range of dates.

Organizing a Group Project with Bento

IN THIS CHAPTER

- Planning the Group Project 177
- One Person = One Project 179
- One Person = Many Projects 184
- One Project = Many People 186
- Many People = Many Projects 187

Planning the Group Project

This chapter shows how to use Bento to manage group projects to keep track of projects and the people who work on them. The chapter approaches projects from the perspective of people working on them. The basic records in Chapters 10 and 11 are for the project, whereas in this chapter, there is always a basic record for a person. As you will see, there may also be related records for projects, but in some cases that data is contained within the record for a person.

➔ The basics of related records are explored in Chapter 7, "Expanding the Inventory Library with Related Records and Collections," p. 98. Chapter 10, "Working with Bento's Projects Library to Use Related Records from iCal Tasks, iCal Events, and Address Book," p. 139, and Chapter 11, "Designing a Projects Library with Related Notes," p. 151, both approach projects from the project side.

Bento is a single-user database, so it is not going to replace a multi-user networked database such as FileMaker Pro. But there are a number of ways in which you can use Bento to coordinate a group project; this chapter explores several of them.

You will also see how to use related records and Bento 2 to integrate group projects even more closely with Address Book and iCal than you have seen before. These techniques can be applied to many Bento projects.

There are several ways to organize a group project. The options available to you have nothing to do with Bento. They are characteristics of all group projects. These organization options include the following:

- In some cases, each member of the group needs to complete something. This is the case for a class in which each student needs to write a report, create an art project, and the like. The number of people in the group is the same as the number of projects to be created. (In database parlance, this is a *one-to-one relationship* between people and projects.)

- There also are cases in which a group member can work on more than one project, but only one person can work on a single project. This is called a *one-to-many relationship* (one group member to many projects).

- In other cases, a project can have more than one person working on it, but an individual can work on no more than one project. This is a *one-to-many relationship* from the project side (one project to many people).

- There are also hybrid projects in which a number of tasks need to be done; each one can have one or more members of the group assigned to it. From the standpoint of the group members, each member can have one or more projects assigned. This type of relationship is a *many-to-many relationship*.

You do not need to know database theory to use Bento, but this particular aspect of database theory, called *cardinality*, is an important point to consider. When you are putting two pieces of data together, stop for a moment and consider the cardinality. Here is how this aspect can play out in Bento:

- For one-to-one relationships, you can put all the data in a single record. If each person works on a project and there is no sharing, one record can hold everything. You will see how to use Bento to display parts of the data in separate forms.

- For one-to-many relationships, the normal way of handling this in Bento is to create a second library for the many sides of the relationship (as in "one-to-many") and to create a list of related records as you have seen previously in this book. If one person can work on several projects, an individual record will have a related records list that displays projects from another library. If a project can have many people working on it, the one side of the structure is the project, and the related list is for the people who are working on it.

- For many-to-many relationships, you simply follow the examples shown in Chapter 12, "Building a Garden/Nature Log." Create bidirectional relationships just as you did for Garden Log to Crop and then for Crops back to Garden Log. In Bento 2, using "hot relations" with the go to related record icon at the lower left of the related records list field lets you switch from Garden Log and its related Crops records to Crops and its related Garden Log records. In a sense, neither library is primary: each uses the other as its own related records.

TIP

Some database designers always start by looking for the "one"—the side of the relationship that can have only one element. Not all relationships have a one side, but if you find a relationship with a one side, you can treat it differently and more simply than a many side.

One Person = One Project

A common example of the One Person = One Project structure is a class in which each student works on a project. The Student List library that is built into Bento is a good place to start. Figure 13.1 shows the Student List library's table view, and Figure 13.2 shows the form view of that library.

Figure 13.1

The Student List table view shows each record in a single line.

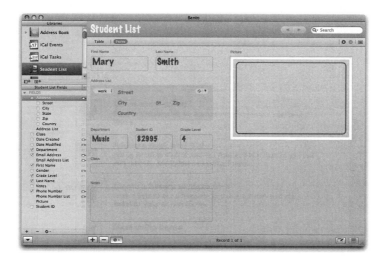

Figure 13.2

The default form view in Student List displays a single record in the window.

If each student has a single project (and vice versa), there is no reason to create new records or a new library. The project information can go in the existing records. If you want, you can add some project information to the table view. You can also add project information to the form view, but you might prefer to create a new view specifically for the project.

What additional information is needed depends on the type of projects you are tracking. You might need a field to keep track of a grade for the project. You might want a field that contains a description of the project. Files associated with the project might also be useful.

You can also use the techniques described in Chapter 11, "Designing a Projects Library with Related Notes," to create related records for the project. These could be any list of items for the project such as notes, materials, or progress reports.

Create a New Form

In Bento, the simplest way to do this is to start from the default form in the Student List. Then choose Insert > Duplicate Form to make a copy of the original form. It will be indistinguishable from the original form (except that its name will have Copy at the end). Now is a good time to rename it and also to rename the original form; good names are Student Form and Project View.

In the duplicate form, delete all the fields that you do not need for the project. You might want to leave only the student name, but you may need the class and some additional information to disambiguate duplicate names. Figure 13.3 shows what the project form might look like now.

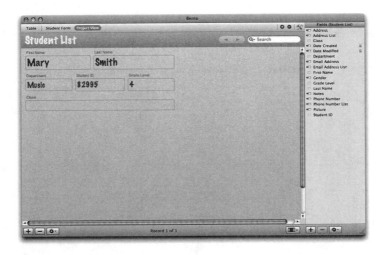

Figure 13.3

Delete unneeded fields from the project form.

NOTE

As noted previously, this deletion process is greatly facilitated if you keep the data you will need on multiple forms in the top of the default form so that when it is duplicated, that data will be in the same place. If it is in the bottom part of the form, the fields will automatically slide up. Working with multiple forms is much easier if the same data is always in the same place on each one within a Bento library.

Now all you have to do is decide what information about the project you want to appear on every form. Depending on what it is, many possibilities could come to mind:

- Project name
- Date due
- Status (perhaps a choice field with a popup menu of values such as Not Started, In Progress, and Complete)
- Grade (if this is a school project)
- Notes

Add a File List Field

There are two more possible sets of project data you could incorporate into Bento. If the project consists of one or more files, you can add those files to the project in a file list field, as shown in Figure 13.4. (Note that this is a file list field, not a related records list.)

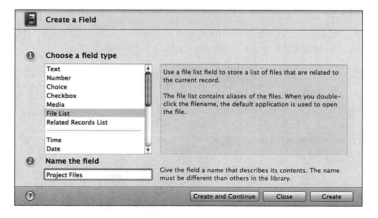

Figure 13.4

Add a project files field.

These files can be anywhere that you can access them; they could be on a server to which you and your students have access. Double-clicking a file in the file list opens it (provided that you have an application that can read that file type). Using a file list field is a good solution if the project has many files. If the project will consist of a single file (a movie, perhaps), instead of a file list field, you might opt for a media field.

Figure 13.5 shows one way in which you can add a file list field to the Project View form. Because of Bento's deep integration with Mac OS X, file list fields can become a powerful tool in your Bento libraries. You can create lists of files and, with the buttons at the bottom left of the field, click to open a selected file or click to show it in a Finder window.

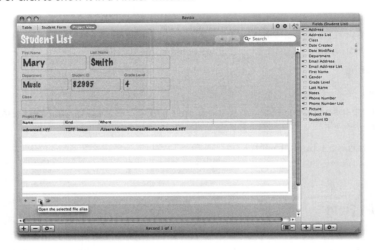

Figure 13.5
Add a file list field.

In Bento 2, an additional icon is found at the lower left of the file list field. It opens the selected file in Mac OS X Quick Look, as shown in Figure 13.6.

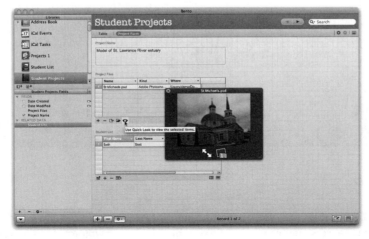

Figure 13.6
Use Quick Look to look inside a file in a file list.

Notice that the file list field has been enlarged horizontally and vertically from the default size. The filename can become lengthy, and widening that column can help to identify the file. When you do that, you may consider moving from a default two-column layout to a single column layout so that the entire file list field can be wider.

TIP

When you are working on large projects and big databases, the advice has always been to plan as much as possible in advance because the cost of making changes is significant. (Even if you are doing the work for yourself, the cost is your time.) With tools like Bento, that advice no longer applies. Just create your project, see if it looks right, and if it doesn't, try again. Because you can modify the Bento forms at any time, you can even use a form for months or years before deciding that you want to invest a minute or two in a change.

Organize Your Files

There are now four basic ways to organize files on your Mac. At various times you may use any of them; they are not mutually exclusive.

The first type of organization is the traditional Finder file/folder structure. Files are placed within folders that then may be placed within other folders all the way to your home directory and from there (because it, too, is a folder) to the root of your hard disk. The file/folder structure has been extended with aliases and Smart Folders, both of which let you work with a reference to a file; thus, the file can appear to be in two places at the same time. The principle behind this type of organization is the *location* where something is stored.

The second type of organization is based on *applications*. Most applications support an Open Recent command in their File menu; they may also provide their own directories of files that you have opened with the application. After you have launched an application that you regularly use (one of the iWork applications, for example), you can quickly open the presentations, spreadsheets, or documents that you have previously worked on. This is application-based file management.

A third type of organization is provided by *Spotlight*. You can use Spotlight to search for files based on their characteristics and even their content. But there is another part of Spotlight that many people do not use. You can proactively provide comments about a file that Spotlight can retrieve. Thus, you can organize your files by location (the first method) or by your own codes and categories (Spotlight). To provide Spotlight comments, select the file or folder in question, choose File > Get Info and enter the Spotlight comments as shown in Figure 13.7.

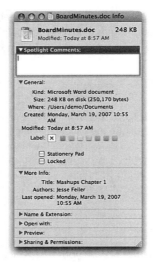

Figure 13.7
Add Spotlight comments to files and folders.

Finally, and most powerfully, you have *Bento's file organization*. Files are just one part of a bigger picture—a project, a list, a set of ideas, your vacation, or whatever you have in your Bento library. There are certainly times when you want to browse files in other ways (your photos, for example, no matter what they are related to), but for many people, being able to quickly get to files and folders associated with a specific item is invaluable. With Bento, the files and folders as well as other information are all together. When you decide to work on that project or relax with your vacation plans, you do not have to go searching for files.

Collecting files into a Bento file list provides a more sophisticated type of organization that fits right into Bento's organization of Address Book entries, iCal events and tasks, and Mail messages that you add to specific Bento records.

One Person = Many Projects

The One Person = Many Projects structure is a classic use of related records. You can use some of the same ideas described previously in creating a new library for related records, each one of which is a project.

The Student List library so far contains records for students and the projects they work on in the one-to-one structure described in the preceding section. If one person can work on many projects, you need to do a little restructuring. The first step is simple: create a new library called Student Projects. It can be based on the Projects library template, or it can be a blank library to which you add the fields you need.

Review the Student List library to see which fields are related to projects, not students. If you have followed the example in this chapter, the only field that is related solely to a project is the Project Files field. Add such a field to the new Student Projects library. Because there is no longer a one-to-one relationship between students and projects, you cannot identify a project by a student's name; that means you need a name for each project. In addition, if you have added fields or related records for materials, comments, or a project grade, those now need to be added to the Student Projects library and removed from the Student List library.

Figure 13.8 shows what the Student Projects library could look like now.

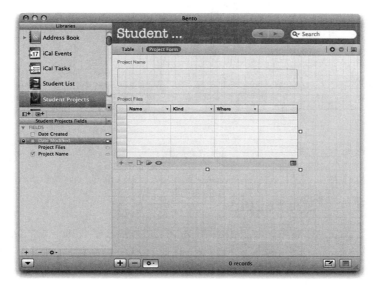

Figure 13.8

Create the library for related records.

See Chapter 15, "Importing and Exporting Bento Data and Libraries," p. 206, for a faster way of splitting a library into two parts using Bento 2.

Then all you need to do is to add a related records field to the Student List library and choose your new library. Figure 13.9 shows what the Student List might look like now. It is quite similar to the layout shown previously, but in this case, instead of multiple files for a single project, there are multiple related projects, each of which has its own file list.

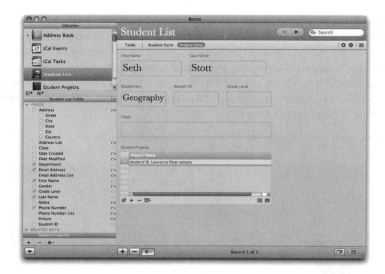

Figure 13.9
Add a related records field.

One Project = Many People

The One Project = Many People structure uses the same basic approach as the preceding example. The only difference here is that instead of starting with the one side (the person) and creating the related records (the projects), you start with the Student List library, which is the many side of the relationship. So in this case, you need to create a Project library and relate the Student List to it.

You can use the Student List and Project library from the preceding section to do this. All you need to do is to add a related records field for Student List to the Project library, and you have it set up, as shown in Figure 13.9.

Follow the same steps to create a Student Projects library; delete project-related fields from the Student List library and add them to the Student Projects library. However, instead of relating Student Projects to Student List, relate Student List to Student Projects so that the related records list field is in Student Projects, not Student List, as shown in Figure 13.10. (Note that the Project Files field, which looks like a related records list field, is in Student Projects along with the related records list field for Student List. A given project needs to have both its students and its files shown.)

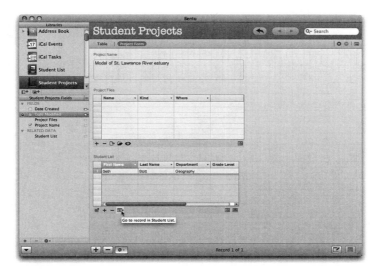

Figure 13.10

Create a multiperson project.

Many People = Many Projects

Many People = Many Projects is the simplest task of all. To create a many-to-many relationship, simply implement both of the previous sections. Create the new Student Projects library and relate it to Student List with a related records list field in Student List. Then relate Student List to Student Projects, with a related records list field in Student Projects. In Bento 2, you are able to flip back and forth by going to the related records with the icon at the lower left of the related records list field.

Creating a Storyboard
with Bento

IN THIS CHAPTER

■ Planning the Storyboard   189

■ Creating the Storyboard
Library   192

Planning the Storyboard

This chapter and Chapter 16, "Managing an Email List from Constant Contact or Vertical Response with Bento," explore specific uses of Bento that go beyond the most common examples. You can use them as-is, or you can use them as models for your own storyboard and email lists or for other projects that have similarities.

Managing Complexity with Bento

Bento is a personal database that is not designed for networking or for multiple users, but that does not mean that it cannot handle complexity. (Databases are designed for handling complexity as well as large volumes of data.)

Many complex problems that are managed with databases have aspects of complexity that are not suited for Bento. That said, there are types of complexity that Bento can handle, making it an ideal tool if that happens to be what you are dealing with. The major issues have to do with related records (which is where most issues with modern databases occur).

RELATIONS AND DATABASES

Almost all databases today are relational databases; at their core is a technology called *SQL*. Data is stored in *tables* that look like spreadsheets. Each *row* is a data record, and each *column* is a field of data (such as name or miles-per-gallon). Under the hood, database designers manipulate the data using *queries* written in SQL. A query gets certain specified data from a table. It also can *join* two tables so that the query matches up a name in one table with a name in another so that a person's data can be drawn at runtime from two different tables. It is this joining of data using a *relationship* (the name in one table with the name in another table) that gives the entire technology the name *relational database*.

In products such as FileMaker Pro, queries, as such, do not exist. A more developer-friendly interface is provided, and you can use it to specify relationships between and among the FileMaker Pro tables. In most other relational databases, the relationships are dynamically related in queries rather than being specified explicitly as they are in FileMaker Pro. This section discusses relationships in the Bento and FileMaker Pro sense, but they exist dynamically in other database products such as MySQL.

The fact that Bento does not handle certain types of complexity is a comment, not a criticism. The Bento developers have carefully laid out an incredibly useful tool that does truly bring databases to "the rest of us." In the world of technology, any tool that provides innovation and simplicity often is criticized for what it leaves out. For many years, programmers criticized databases because they hid the underlying file access mechanism, and the programmers could no longer read and write to the database. In more advanced tools such as FileMaker Pro and even Bento, some users even complain about the same thing: they cannot save their data because FileMaker Pro or Bento automatically does it. Some people would rather explicitly save a file when they want to (and when they think about it) rather than have the software automatically save it for them. For the vast majority of users, the fact that Bento saves automatically and saves its data in a known place is an advantage. Other people want to control not only the saving of the data but also the location of the data.

In this section, some of the issues that Bento does not handle are discussed mostly so that you can decide right at the start if your idea is right for Bento or if you need to restructure that idea or even use another tool. Also, you will see how Bento handles certain types of complexity, which can mean that a project you thought might require a different type of tool may be one that you can implement quickly and easily using Bento.

Bento excels at bringing organization to sets of data that may consist of many records but where the individual records are not complex. For example, you have seen how you can modify the built-in Inventory library by relating an in/out library to it. The in/out library may contain a date and some descriptive information about the transaction, but it is a simple yet necessary component of your inventory system.

In Chapter 13, "Organizing a Group Project with Bento," you saw how you could use related records and file lists to organize projects and students. Again, this capability shows Bento's simplicity. The related records can be shown in a related records field, with one line for each related record; you can have as many columns as you want, but you are practically constrained by the width of the window and display. This means that, in a practical sense, a related records field cannot display more than about half a dozen fields from the related record. If the related record contains 50 fields, you have to choose which few fields you want to display.

In Bento 2, you can click on the icon at the bottom left of a related records list field to go to the selected record where you can see its fields in a form view. Even so, there is a constraint, because a single form view cannot be larger than the screen unless you use the scrollbars.

A Bento form view is elegant and customizable with the Bento interface tools. But there are some things you cannot do. If you are used to traditional databases, you may see that you can only display related records in a related records field, which means that implementing a one-to-one relationship (where, for example, you have a single job assignment record for a single employee) requires you to use a scrolling list of all the related records (which will always be one). In a tool such as FileMaker Pro, you can develop an interface (*layout* in FileMaker Pro terms) where the fields come from the basic record as well as from related records, and nothing in the interface appearance or behavior tells the user which ones are local and which are related. This ability to make related records indistinguishable in the layout from local records, which is something you cannot do in Bento, may appear to make the interface simpler, but it complicates the design and implementation.

There are two other relationship concerns. The first is bidirectional relationships. As you saw in Chapter 13, you can relate students to projects, and you can also relate projects to students. You can implement a bidirectional relationship by creating a students-to-projects relationship and a projects-to-students relationship. The only thing to be careful about is that once relating A to B, relate B to A rather than accidentally relating C to A.

Finally, relationships in Bento have only one "hop." You can relate A to B, and you can relate B to C, but that does not imply a relationship from A to C through B as it would in FileMaker Pro. Using the Chapter 13 example, you can create related records for a project that contain materials needed for that project. If you relate the project to a student record, the student record can display the project, but the student record cannot display the related materials for the project, because the materials are two "hops" away.

The preceding are some of the issues of complexity that can be problematic in Bento. But what does Bento handle well when it comes to complexity? As it turns out, the relationships that Bento implements are a tremendous advantage for a project such as storyboards. The basic storyboard contains two types of information: single data values (such as a name) and multiple data values (such as lists of costumes, actors, sets, and so forth). This is the type of complexity that Bento handles brilliantly. Because the actual structuring of the Bento database is so simple to do, changing that structure by replacing a field with a related records list field is simple.

NOTE

If you think having multiple values within a field is not a common problem with databases and the applications that are built on them, look at the databases in which multiple phone numbers are squeezed into a single field (which can cause an interface that automatically dials a number to fail because the field contains two numbers).

In a traditional database, implementing a multitude of relationships for a given record can introduce complexity and performance issues. In Bento, in part because the relationships are so much simpler, you can implement as many relationships as you want in a record without worrying.

Learning About Storyboards

Storyboards started as comic strip-like drawings that provided a basic visual representation of each scene in a movie (both live action as well as animated). They now are also routinely used for describing other sequences of basically visual events: commercials, website navigation, DVD menus, and games, among others.

Through advances in technology, Jose Marti's statement in the mid-1800s, "in the future, photographers will populate the world" seems to have come true, and to have been extended to movie making as well as still photos. With tools such as iPhoto, iMovie, and iDVD in Apple's iLife suite as well as professional tools such as Aperture and FinalCut Pro, you can create amazing results. Whether you are working on a video designed for training, an advocacy website, a movie that is a costume epic reenactment of the Battle of Plattsburgh, or a family history, organizing it with a storyboard before you start shooting will save you time and money. As anyone who has worked on an advertising commercial can tell you, a 10-second spot can entail what seems to be as much effort as the preparations to shoot a major motion picture. In fact, being brief is often much more difficult than being lengthy.

Bento is ideally suited to be a tool to construct storyboards because it is easy to use and because it so easily integrates media into your library. The media integration, along with the integration of any files to which you have access, lets you pull your storyboard together quickly. Also, Bento's remarkably simple method of relating records in other libraries means that your Bento storyboard library can be the heart of your project. You can even incorporate research for a family history into the storyboard itself.

The following section provides one way of approaching the storyboard project. You can use it as-is, but you can also use it as a jumping-off point for your own variations. In abstract terms, this is a Bento library of ordered information (the individual scenes of the storyboard), each of which may have any number of related records associated with it.

Creating the Storyboard Library

Each record in the storyboard library consists of a frame of the storyboard. Many storyboards consist simply of a sketch of what the scene will look like. The sketch generally implies a camera angle, and it shows an overview or key moment from the action of that frame. As time and technology have moved on, storyboards have grown to incorporate more data, digital images instead of sketches, and sometimes video clips that illustrate what will eventually be shot. During production, it is even possible to replace an initial sketch with a draft of video and then with final video so that the storyboard can, if you want, morph into the finished product.

NOTE

In reality, revisions often occur as production goes on. Furthermore, there are usually multiple takes of a given scene so that a given frame of a storyboard may actually have a multitude of takes from which to choose.

This example relies on a multitude of related record fields that are easy to create and use in Bento. Whereas in many Bento libraries there are only a few related record fields (if any), in this library, there are six related record fields to 10 single-value fields. If more fields were to be added to the database, they would probably be related record fields as noted in the sections that follow.

Implementing the Single-Value Fields

For each frame of the storyboard, fields identify the frame and provide basic information about it. These are the single-value fields along with their meanings and field types:

- **Title (text):** This is what you call this storyboard frame. The title does not need to be unique but should provide some clue as to what it is. If the script identifies scenes with a naming or numbering scheme, that is what you should use. In fact, if you have a numbering scene in the script, you may choose to add the scene number as its own field.

- **Sequence (number):** One of the advantages of a database-driven storyboard is that you can rearrange the frames as you go along. Thus, each frame has a sequence number. You can start out with 1, 2, 3, and so forth. As you develop the storyboard, you may realize you need an intermediate frame between 1 and 2: just give it a sequence number of 1.5. Furthermore, if you realize that 3 might actually go between 1 and the new 1.5, just number it 1.3. Remember that there are always numbers between any two real numbers. (Bento basically does not care how many decimal places you use.) You may wind up with the first four sequence numbers being 1, 2, 2.2, and 2.4.

- **Status (choice):** This lets you keep track of work with popup values of In Progress, Storyboard Complete, and Project Complete.

- **Length (duration):** This starts with the estimated duration of the scene but can be refined as you actually shoot the movie.

- **Image (media):** This can be a digital photo, a movie, a scanned image of a sketch on the back of an envelope that you have subsequently scanned, or any visual about the frame.

- **Notes (text).**

- **Time (text):** This is the time of day for the scene: it might be 2 p.m., or it might be morning, or it might be two years later. This information comes from the script. It is a text field because you may need to use "times," such as "morning."

- **Setting (text):** This information also comes from the script, and it describes where the scene takes place.

- **Place (choice):** This lets you choose where the scene will be shot: on location, on a set, or as a digital special effect.

- **Script (text):** Because Bento text fields can handle very large amounts of text, you can actually paste the text of the scene from the script into this field.

- Other possible fields could include the cost of this particular frame, the individual responsible, and checkboxes indicating special conditions such as night-time shooting, children, animals, and the like.

With these fields created, you can choose some of them for the table view. Figure 14.1 shows Sequence, Title, Status, and Length in the table view. Note that Sequence is sorted so that the frames come out in the right order. Notice also that the Length field is summed up in the Summary Row so that you can see how long the total piece will be. (Bento's duration field handles the conversions from seconds and minutes and hours so that you can enter the data in the most logical format and the sum is still correct.)

NOTE

It is important that the sequence field be a number. If it is a text field, it is not sorted properly. In Figure 14.1, a text Sequence field has been created, and the data is sorted on that field in ascending order, which means that 10 appears between 1.7 and 2 because it is "alphabetized" based on the values of the characters. If the sequence field that is a number is sorted, it works properly.

Remember that you can use fields in the record that are not shown in the table view for searching. If you want to search for location frames, just type location into the search box.

Figure 14.1

Implement the table view.

Implementing the Related Record Fields

Now you can implement a number of related record fields. Each related record stores structure information about one separate aspect of the storyboard frame.

Figure 14.2 shows six related record fields for characters, costumes (or wardrobe), props, tasks, events, and people. The last three use built-in iCal and Address Book data. You can implement this library in either Bento 1 or Bento 2, but Figure 14.2 shows Bento 2. The new go to related record icon at the bottom of each related records list field is a powerful addition.

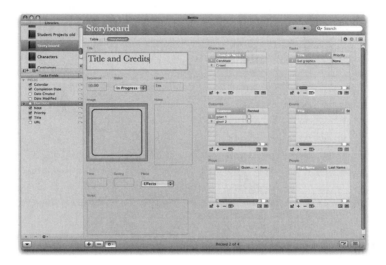

Figure 14.2

Implement the form view.

Other possible related fields for a storyboard could be used to track crew members (even if the choice is between you and your brother), vehicles to be used in the scene, and special equipment (such as a fan hidden behind a tree to guarantee a flapping flag). Anything that applies to a frame of the storyboard and that might come in more than one instance belongs in a related record field. You could lump everything together in a notes field, but the more you structure your data for a storyboard or for any Bento database, the easier it is to enter and find things.

Yes, structuring the data makes entry easier. The reason is that, as soon as you build a structure for entering data, you can not only see it, but can also notice immediately if something is blank. In jumbled-together notes fields, you have to stop and think whether you've remembered everything. With related records fields to fill in (or to add from the related records database), you are prompted to think of each type of related record.

You can use the techniques described in Chapter 13 to implement the second half of the relation-ships. For example, there is a relationship from Storyboard to Characters, as shown in Figure 14.2. If you implement a relationship from Characters to Storyboard and place a related records list field in Characters that displays the Storyboard record, you can see the other side of the relationship, as shown in Figure 14.3.

Figure 14.3

All the storyboard frames in which a specific character appears.

Implementing Related Record Fields in iCal and Address Book

You create relationships in the same way for iCal Tasks and Events as well as Address Book. With the data shown in Figure 14.3, clicking on the go to related records button in the Tasks related records list field sends you to the record shown in Figure 14.4. (In Bento 1, you manually need to go to that record in the iCal Tasks library.)

Remember that iCal Tasks and Events as well as Address Book are special libraries that link directly to the data in iCal and Address Book. But remember, too, that you can create additional fields in these libraries. The additional fields are just for Bento: they are not synchronized to iCal or Address Book, but you can use them. Thus, you can create a related records list field in the iCal Tasks library that is related to Storyboard. Thus, the tasks, events, and people-related records function is the same as those in libraries that you create, as shown in Figure 14.5.

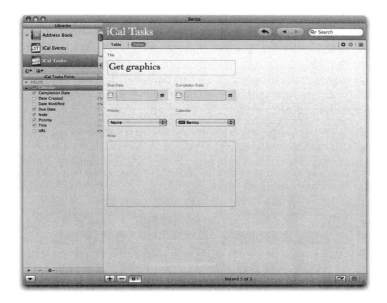

Figure 14.4
Go to a related record in iCal Tasks.

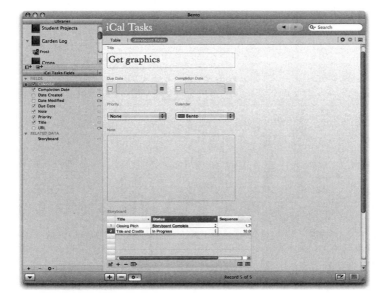

Figure 14.5
You can create related records list fields in iCal Tasks and Events as well as Address Book.

Moving Forward

The next steps are likely to be further iterations of the previous steps: adding new fields to the libraries, and, frequently, adding new libraries to be related to existing ones. In such a structure, the primary related libraries all show up in the main library (Storyboard). If they have their own related libraries (materials, notes, and so forth), they show up only when you go to the related library; they are not visible in the main (Storyboard) library.

This structure is simple and powerful, and it keeps each library small and focused. You can apply this structure to any number of Bento projects.

A variety of small libraries are shown in Chapter 17, "Bento Quickies," p. 225. You can use them as-is or as suggestions for auxiliary libraries that you can add onto your own Bento libraries.

15

Importing and Exporting Bento Data and Libraries

IN THIS CHAPTER

- Importing and Exporting Basics   199

- Importing and Exporting Libraries   206

Importing and Exporting Basics

One of the key features of Bento is the ease with which data can be imported and exported. In Chapter 4, "Building a Bento Library from Your Own Data," you saw how to take a data file and import it into Bento, automatically creating a new table from the data. It is a simple process that can quickly bring legacy data, data from the Web, or any other data in a supported format into Bento.

In Bento 1, the sole supported import format was a comma-separated-value (CSV) file. This is a standard file type that is widely available, particularly in spreadsheet applications. With Bento 2, the support formats now include spreadsheets from Excel and Numbers as well as tab-delimited files such as those from AppleWorks. And, as noted in Chapter 4, if you happen to have data that is in yet another format, you frequently can export it in an intermediate format to a third application and, from there, save it or export it in a supported format.

This chapter expands on Chapter 4 by showing you how to import data into an existing library; it also shows you how to export data from Bento. Then, in the second part of the chapter you see how to use a major new feature in Bento 2: the ability to export not just the data but an entire Bento library including its forms.

Importing Data into an Existing Bento Library

Importing data has a number of variations:

- You may have a Bento table with no data and you want to import data from an external file.

- Your Bento table may have some data already and you want to add data with your import.

- Your Bento table may or may not have some data, and it may have some fields. With your import, you want to add new fields and data for them.

The process described in this section applies to all the variations.

The example used in this section is a familiar task for authors and editors of books: it can be summed up in the question, "How is the page count coming?" In addition to all the other considerations of writing a book, this is something that needs to be managed so that the book comes in on target. Because books are usually written with word processing software such as Microsoft Word or Pages, and because the figures and illustrations are created separately from the text, it is important to find a way to approximate the number of printed pages in each chapter.

For many book layouts, a simple formula is used:

- One word processing page is approximately one laid-out page in a book. (In fact, many authors and publishers use word processing styles that have fonts, font size, and margins that make this approximation more accurate. A page typed in Helvetica 42 will not wind up being anywhere close to a laid-out page in a standard book font.)

- One figure with its caption, figure number, and white-space margins above and below is approximately half a laid-out page.

For a book of several hundred pages, this formula is reasonably accurate, at least for the purposes of tracking page count until the pages are actually laid out. For any individual page, it may be somewhat off. Authors and editors frequently keep track of page count with a spreadsheet, such as the one shown in Figure 15.1. Note that the Total column is a calculation.

Figure 15.1

Page count data in an Excel spreadsheet.

The first scenario is the most basic: Import data from the external data source into a Bento table with no data. The Bento table is set up, as shown in Figure 15.2.

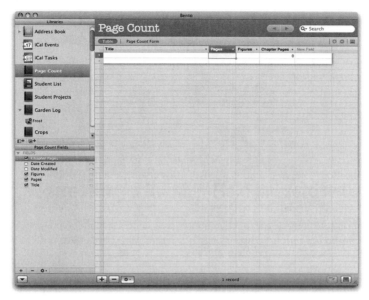

Figure 15.2

Create the Bento table.

Title is a text field; Pages and Figures are number fields. The Chapter Pages field is a calculation field (shown in Figure 15.3).

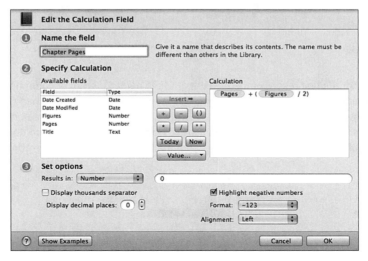

Figure 15.3

Use a calculation for the Chapter Pages field.

Choose File > Import > File to open the Import dialog, as shown in Figure 15.4.

New In Bento 2, after you choose the file to import, you are able to choose the delimiter if it is a CSV file.

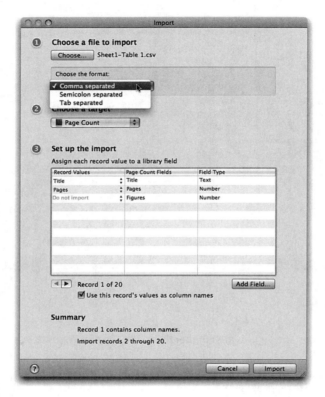

Figure 15.4

Select import settings.

If Bento senses that the first record of the file contains field names (Bento) or column headings (spreadsheet), it attempts to match them. Figure 15.4 shows that Bento has declined to import anything into the Figures field. If you compare Figures 15.1 and 15.2, you see that the Bento Figures field logically matches the spreadsheet Figs field. Because the match is not exact, Bento does not import the data by default. However, you can use the popup menu to refine the import settings, as shown in Figure 15.5.

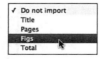

Figure 15.5

Modify field import settings.

TIP

You can also use the double-headed arrows to rearrange the sequence of the imported fields.

As pointed out in Chapter 4, you can adjust the starting record and decide if you want the starting record to be used as titles. Figure 15.6 shows an import specification that uses no title record and starts at record 7.

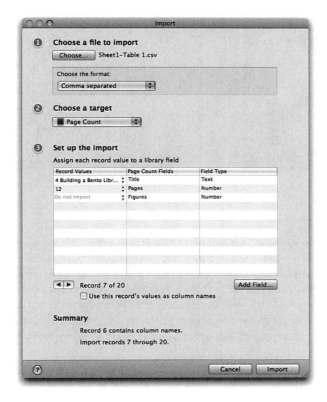

Figure 15.6

Select import settings.

Figure 15.7 shows the imported data.

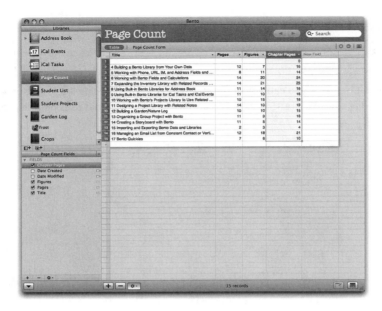

Figure 15.7

Select import settings.

In Bento 2, you can also copy and paste data into a Bento table view. Select the part of the spreadsheet you want to use and then copy it to the Clipboard as you normally would do. Then, in the Bento table view, click in the cell that you want to be the upper left of the imported data. Then, paste the data. Rows and columns can then be added manually as needed. In most cases, you do not want to add columns in this way, so the upper left cell of your imported data is in the appropriate column (that is, a Pages spreadsheet cell in the Pages column of the blank row of the Bento table view). If there are discrepancies, you are asked what to do, as shown in Figure 15.8.

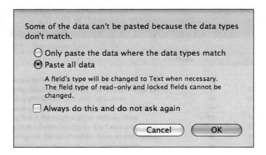

Figure 15.8

Tell Bento what to do about field data conflicts.

Exporting Bento Data

In Bento 1, choose File > Export to export a CSV file from the current library.

In Bento 2, exporting data from Bento has many more options. The first thing to notice is that the File > Export dialog now contains many more options, as shown in Figure 15.9.

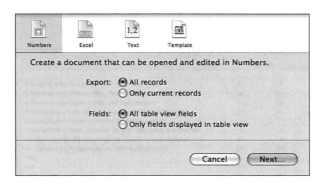

Figure 15.9

Bento 2 has a number of export options.

Whether you are exporting to Numbers, Excel, or a text file, your first choice is whether to select all records in the Bento library or just the current records (those you have found as the result of a search). In addition, you can choose to export all the library's fields or just those shown in the table view. If you are exporting text data, you can choose the delimiter, as shown in Figure 15.10.

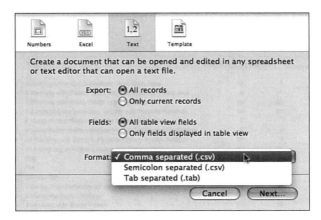

Figure 15.10

Choose the delimiter for text data exports.

In Bento 1, the only export format is CSV, but you can change the export delimiter. That choice is made in Bento > Preferences.

NOTE

Related records are not exported from Bento.

Importing and Exporting Libraries

New One of the most requested additional features in Bento 1 was the capability to import and export libraries (not just their data). That request has been fulfilled in Bento 2.

Exporting Bento Libraries as Templates

Exporting a Bento library as a template starts with File > Export. Choose the Template tab at the top to open the dialog, as shown in Figure 15.11.

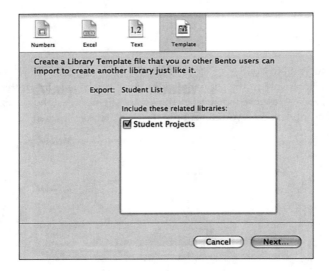

Figure 15.11

Export a Bento library.

Unlike exporting to a file, when you export a Bento library template, you can include related tables. When you have selected any related tables, click Next; you are asked to select a name for the file, and that is all you have to do.

Importing Bento Libraries as Templates

Importing is just as easy. Choose File > Import > Template. The library (or libraries) are imported into Bento, and you can start to use them right away.

16

Managing an Email List from Constant Contact or Vertical Response with Bento

IN THIS CHAPTER

- Learning About Email Lists and Bulk Email   207

- Using a Vendor to Send Bulk Email   211

- Moving Your Bento Email Library to and from a Vendor   213

Learning About Email Lists and Bulk Email

You can manage anything with Bento: contacts (including email addresses), recipes, projects, or software registration codes. For many people, managing an email list is one of the tasks that springs to mind as soon as the word "database" is uttered. Whether it is for a periodic newsletter to friends and family, for a list of events in the community, or for news of specials in the weekly farmers' market, an email list is a great way of communicating with people. Bento can be a valuable tool in managing that list, but it is not the only one available.

This chapter shows you not only how to use Bento but also how and why to use email services to work with Bento to manage your mailing list.

To live in the world of email lists, you need to know your way around issues such as spam because your Bento library is going to have to track items that will make your messages deliverable when sent in bulk.

Communicating with Multiple People

When you want to broadcast information to a group of people on the Internet, you can accomplish your goal in three primary ways:

- You can send email to the people you want to reach. You can do this in separately addressed emails, an email with a number of cc or bcc recipients, or an email to a predefined group. (In that case, your email application typically converts it into separate emails.)

- You can publish the information on a website or blog so that anyone who knows the address or finds it in a search engine can see what you have to say.

- You can combine a web publication with a technology such as Atom or RSS. (Most blogging software automatically supports this technology.) Users then subscribe to your news feed, and their browser or email application alerts them to changes you have made to your published information on the Web.

- In addition, discussion groups on social networking sites such as Facebook or sites such as Google or Yahoo! allow people to talk among themselves and sometimes send messages to the entire group.

Sending email puts you in charge: you send the messages when you want to and to whom you want to. (Of course, people need not read them and may not even receive them if they are trapped by spam filters.) This is what is called a *push* technology.

The second method relies totally on your potential readers and viewers checking your website or blog; although you play a key role by publishing the information, it is their request for the information that brings it to them. This is known as a *pull* technology.

The third method is a composite. It is the user's email program, web browser, or newsreader that does the pulling, but that is in response to a request by the user to set it up (perhaps just by clicking a link that the application stores for routine updates).

Depending on what your message is and with whom you are communicating, any of these strategies (or a combination of them) may be right for you. Perhaps because email gives the sender the most control, many people like to use it. If you are sending multiple messages, you can use Bento to manage the mailing list.

Knowing Your Way Around Bulk Email (Spam)

Email is one of the great innovations of the last half-century. Its roots go back to ARPAnet, the predecessor of the Internet, which dates from the late 1960s. (It first went live on November 21, 1969.) The first email message was sent in 1971, and by 1973, 75% of ARPAnet traffic was email. Before long, unsolicited email messages from strangers began to flood email in-boxes and acquired the name *spam* in a roundabout route through a famous sketch on *Monty Python's Flying Circus*. The first spam message was probably sent in 1978, and the first massive commercial email message was sent on April 12, 1994. Since that time, the volume of messages has grown more rapidly, straining network resources and annoying many recipients.

NOTE

More formal than the word "spam" are the acronyms "UBE," which means unsolicited bulk email, and "UCE," which means unsolicited commercial email. They reflect the three major characteristics that people identify with spam: it is unsolicited (and usually unwanted), it is sent in bulk (sometimes millions of messages at a time), and it is generally commercial although it can be used to distribute viruses and other malware, to probe for valid email addresses, and for other purposes that are not directly commercial.

If technology was the source of the spam outbreak, it was able to be part of the solution. Today, filters throughout the Internet's email environment attempt to identify spam and either label it appropriately or in some cases simply refuse to forward it to the addressee. This filtering happens all the way from the initial mail server that sends the message through intermediate relayers, to the mail server of the Internet service provider that is the ultimate recipient of the message, and even in desktop email applications. Nevertheless, a great deal of spam does get through, and, occasionally, filters delete legitimate email messages.

In addition to technological solutions and semi-solutions, laws have been passed to attempt to control spam. In the United States, legislation named the "Controlling the Assault of Non-Solicited Pornography and Marketing Act of 2003" was signed by the president, and its acronym, CAN-SPAM, passed into the worlds of marketing and email.

The CAN-SPAM act is triggered when you send email "whose primary purpose is advertising or promoting a commercial product or service, including content on a Web site." It applies to all messages of this kind; you do not have to send millions of them to fall under the CAN-SPAM act. Furthermore, the widespread notion that it does not apply to nonprofits is wrong; it does apply to them if they send email that falls under the definition. As experts in the field like to say, in determining whether a message is spam, it is the content that governs, not the sender.

Knowing Your Way Around Mail Filters

These technical and legal issues all come into play when you send email messages to more than a single person. Spam filters can catch a message and refuse to deliver it or mark it as potential spam. Among the factors that can cause this to happen are these:

- The message contains words, combinations of words, or known combinations of letters that are commonly associated with spam. The people who maintain filters are constantly refining their algorithms to examine messages, and the people who send spam are constantly refining their messages. However, it appears that there is a bit of a decrease in spam in some areas.

- The message is sent from an Internet service provider (ISP) that is known to generate spam and has been blacklisted. Among the issues that can cause blacklisting of this sort are explicit complaints, a large number of returned messages (which can indicate that someone is sending out email to addresses that have not been verified and may even be created at random in what is called a *dictionary attack*), and the like.

- Some filters can identify a particular message that in and of itself might not appear to be spam but, because identically worded messages are sent by the millions within a brief period of time, the apparently innocuous message is flagged as spam and is not delivered.

- If a message contains malware such as a Trojan horse or virus, it may be blocked.

- Along those lines, certain unknown types of attachments to email messages can be flagged as potential malware and cause the messages to be blocked. Sometimes ISPs block messages encrypted using Pretty Good Privacy (PGP) because their digital signatures are flagged as potential malware. (This is perhaps one of the most extreme examples of filtering gone bad.)

There are other considerations, and they keep changing as the ongoing skirmishes between ISPs and spammers continue. For obvious reasons, not all the items that cause email messages to be blocked are disclosed. And, it should be noted, the major mail filtering companies compete with one another to be fastest and most responsive to catching true spam while still allowing legitimate messages.

Knowing Your Way Around ISP Rules

ISPs have a vested interest in not originating spam; if they do so, they run the risk of being blacklisted so that even legitimate users' messages are not delivered. For this reason, as well as the need to manage their traffic, many ISPs impose limits on what you can send. For example, these are the limits in effect at Google's Gmail in the summer of 2008:

- You cannot send a message to more than 500 people; if you use a POP or IMAP client such as Apple Mail, that limit is 100 people.

- If you send "a large number" of undeliverable messages, your account may be disabled. (The number is not specified).

- Reports indicate that there is a limit of 2,000 messages a day for Gmail.

↪   Google provides guidelines for sending bulk email at https://mail.google.com/support/bin/answer.py?answer=81126. Other email providers provide similar guidance although, as is the case with Gmail, they often have subjective limits such as "too many" or "excessive."

Knowing Your Way Around the CAN-SPAM Act

On the legal side, the CAN-SPAM act requires you to obey four rules. (These are in U.S. law; other countries may have similar requirements. In any event, they are not burdensome for legitimate senders.)

- The header information (From and To, for example) must be accurate.

- The subject line must not be misleading.

- The message must contain a valid return address and an opt-out button or link to prevent further emails from being sent. You have 10 days to process the opt-out request, and that link or button must be valid for 30 days after you have sent the original email.

- The message must clearly state that it is an advertisement and that opt-out is available. Furthermore, you must provide the physical address at which you can be contacted (not a postal box).

There is a large set of messages to which most of the law does not apply. Transactional or relationship messages are exempt. As the Federal Trade Commission (FTC) defines them, these are "email that facilitates an agreed-upon transaction or updates a customer in an existing business relationship." You can send email to your customers reminding them that it's time for an oil change; you can also send them unsolicited email updating them on shipping dates or announcing an update to a product they have purchased or expressed interest in.

However, remember that the issues involving filtering are related to but separate from CAN-SPAM compliance. If an ISP decides that your message is spam, it may decline to relay the message, no matter how compliant it is. Likewise, if your message does not comply with the CAN-SPAM act but passes the ISP filtering mechanism, it will be sent.

In sending bulk email, you need to plan for both the filtering issues and CAN-SPAM issues. Fortunately, for the vast majority of small-scale messages you may send to members of a club or customers of a business, you may not have to worry about either issue. But where the boundary line between "small-scale" and other bulk emailings lies is not clear; it is best to take a few sensible precautions that Bento can help you to implement.

 There is more information on the FTC's CAN-SPAM page at http://www.ftc.gov/bcp/conline/pubs/buspubs/canspam.shtm.

Using a Vendor to Send Bulk Email

Because of the issues involved in getting bulk email past mail filters, many individuals, small businesses, nonprofits, and even large businesses turn to vendors that specialize in bulk email. Two of the biggest are Constant Contact and Vertical Response. They have similar features, and each is described in this chapter.

 For more information about Constant Contact, see http://search.constantcontact.com/index.jsp. You can find Vertical Response at http://www.verticalresponse.com.

The two basic reasons for using a bulk email vendor are as follows:

- The vendors have experience with mail filters, and they try to maintain good relationships with the providers of filters. Bulk email vendors allow you to create your own messages, but they are sent from their own mail servers, and they are structured so that they comply with CAN-SPAM requirements such as opt-out links or buttons that they process swiftly, valid headers, and the like. To preserve their good standing with ISPs and other relayers of email, the vendors provide you with tools to test for compliance.

- Your ISP's limits on sending multiple email messages may be low (the Gmail example for Apple Mail is 100 messages a day—too few for many school or church groups even in small communities).

Each of the major vendors provides similar services:

- The capability to maintain and manage email lists on their server or on your own. You can upload and download addresses to and from your computer (and Bento).

- You can pay by the message (Vertical Response) or monthly based on the size of your list (Constant Contact). Prepay discounts are available as well as discounts for nonprofits. The rates are modest.

- Both of these vendors provide the capability to create surveys as well as email.

- Both provide templates that you can customize as well as the capability for you to create your own email messages from scratch. Both then add the CAN-SPAM compliance (opt-out, physical address, and so on).

- They also provide HTML code you can place on your website so that people can click a button and sign up to join your list. That processing is handled by the vendor, and the new names are available the next time you mail. This process can include what is called a *double opt-in mechanism*: someone clicks once to join the list. Then an email is sent to that address, and the user must click a second time (that is the *double* in *double-opt in*). That second click confirms that the email address is valid and that someone with access to that account wants to join the list. Together with opt-out links and buttons, this capability provides the greatest degree of user control over lists to which they subscribe.

- They consolidate addresses so that even if someone is listed twice on your list, only one email is sent to a given address. Furthermore, bounced emails disable that address from future use (but do not delete it from the list).

- They provide enough statistics and analytical reports to satisfy the most metrics-happy user.

- Each provides you with free trials and a wide array of training materials that will help you improve your bulk email (and use more of the service).

TIP

Because these vendors and others offer similar services, and because they allow you to upload and download your lists, you can move from one to the other. For many people, it is worth using Numbers or another spreadsheet to evaluate the size of your list and the number of email messages you may send over the course of a year or other planning period. Although the vendors have different pricing structures, you may find that your planned mailings would cost the same at each, but you may also find that your planned mailings would be substantially more or less expensive under the different pricing structures.

Moving Your Bento Email Library to and from a Vendor

Bulk email vendors generally allow you to upload a file of addresses to be added to your list; you can also download the list in a file. Either file can go into or come from Bento.

In addition, you can manually enter or delete addresses using the vendor's Web interface. Finally, most vendors let you build a form for your website so that people can sign up from there.

No matter what method you use, the file that you download will contain addresses entered from previous uploads, your manual online entry, and users' use of your sign-up form. In a similar vein, the file that you upload goes into your main email file on the vendor's computers along with previously uploaded data, manually entered data, and your users' use of your sign-up form.

Your Bento library may have multiple email addresses. If you are going to use it with bulk email, you need to designate one of them as the bulk email address. That can be a separate field, or you can decide that a certain address such as home address will be the bulk email field.

Also, note one important distinction between Constant Contact and Vertical Response. Vertical Response stores and downloads the record creation date and last modification date, just as Bento does. If you are downloading data from Vertical Response, it is very useful to add two additional Bento fields such as VR Creation and VR Modification to store the dates you receive from Vertical Response. (You cannot update the default Bento creation and modification dates, so you cannot use them to store the Vertical Response creation and modification data.)

Constant Contact has a field for the last add or delete on a record. You can download that information to store in a CC Modification field. (There is no comparable creation field in Constant Contact.)

Uploading Bulk Email Data from Bento

In both Constant Contact and Vertical Response, you need to start by creating your mailing list for your account on their website. After you have done that, you need to export data from your Bento library as a CSV file. Although you do not need to fill in every field in the bulk email database, for the fields that you care about, you need to have a mapping from your Bento library to the bulk email database. Most of the time doing that is simple, but if you are storing multiple email addresses, you need to decide which one will be the bulk email address. Remember that the bulk email vendors do not send duplicates based on email addresses. Someone with the same name and address but two separate email addresses will get two separate bulk emails. For that reason, you may want to consider adding a specific bulk email address to your Bento database.

Also, remember the restrictions described earlier in this chapter. As you will see, during the upload process, you will have to certify that you have fulfilled them.

CAUTION

If you are mingling opt-in and other email addresses in your Bento library, you should seriously consider having one or more fields that identify where the email addresses came from and what, if any, restrictions are placed on them. You will need to certify that your uploaded addresses do not violate the terms of service of the bulk email vendor. If you have exported data from Bento based on a field that lets you know the data is okay to upload, your life is simpler.

After you start sending bulk email, be careful that you handle opt-outs properly. If someone opts out via a bulk email that you have sent, that information will go to the bulk email vendor, and that person will be removed from the list. If someone contacts you directly, you must make certain that you remove that person from the bulk email database. In addition, you must flag him or her in your Bento list as do-not-email. If you leave the blocked record in the bulk email database, you will be okay in most cases: you will upload a duplicate address from time to time, but the bulk email vendor will have the old blocked address and will not send. However, if you have physically removed the record from the bulk email database, the opt-out information will go with it, and you will reinstate the person who opted out. This is both annoying and illegal.

UPLOADING DATA WITH VERTICAL RESPONSE

The process for uploading data in Vertical Response follows:

1. Log in to your Vertical Response account. Click the Lists button on the navigation bar and then the Mailing Lists tab. Find the list to which you want to add Bento data; click Actions and Append Record, as shown in Figure 16.1.

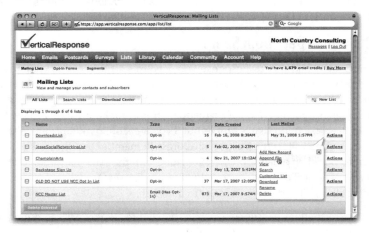

Figure 16.1

Start the upload process in Vertical Response.

2. The next screen you see is the warning shown in Figure 16.2. The bulk email vendors take this seriously; you could lose your account if you abuse the terms.

Figure 16.2

Agree to the terms.

3. Locate your exported Bento CSV file, as shown in Figure 16.3.

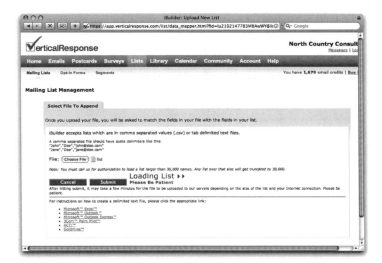

Figure 16.3

Locate the file to upload.

4. The file is uploaded, but it is not yet in the bulk email database. As shown in Figure 16.4, you see the data from the uploaded file; for each column, you can specify which bulk email database field it goes into. You can also choose not to load a specific field. Because you are

seeing the data, you can review the records to see whether anything looks strange. Normally, the Bento CSV output goes without a hitch, but it does not hurt to take a moment to look at the data.

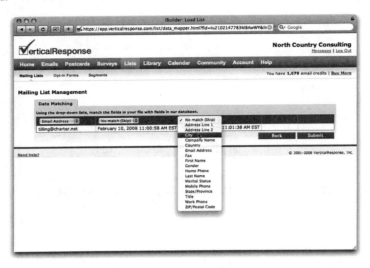

Figure 16.4
Match the uploaded Bento data to the bulk email database fields.

5. After you click Submit, the data is moved into the bulk email database, and you see the report shown in Figure 16.5. If records have been skipped, you can download them to review them. (The download process is the same as the download process described later in this chapter.)

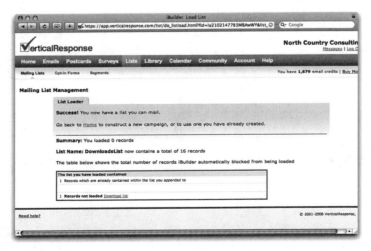

Figure 16.5
Check the upload results.

UPLOADING DATA WITH CONSTANT CONTACT

The process in Constant Contact is much the same:

1. In Constant Contact, go to the Contacts tab, Manage Contacts, and then Add/Import, as shown in Figure 16.6.

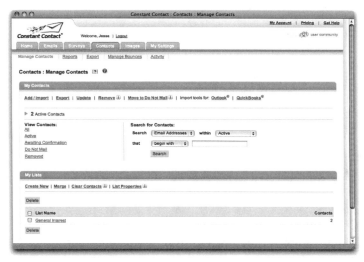

Figure 16.6

Begin the Constant Contact import.

2. Select the list to which you want to import or create a new one, as shown in Figure 16.7.

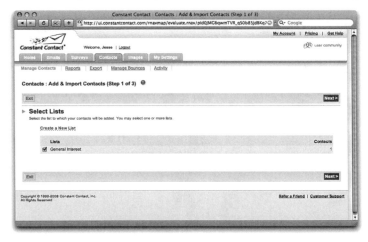

Figure 16.7

Select the list.

3. On the next screen, you have the option of typing in data or importing a file. Choose the option to import data, as shown in Figure 16.8.

Figure 16.8

Choose to import the CSV file.

4. Then, just as with Vertical Response, select the CSV file exported from Bento, as shown in Figure 16.9.

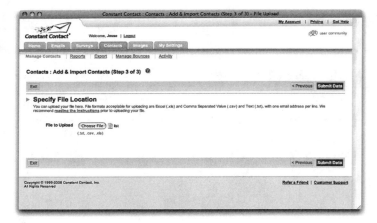

Figure 16.9

Select the CSV file.

5. Next, you need to confirm that you are uploading permission-based names, as shown in Figure 16.10.

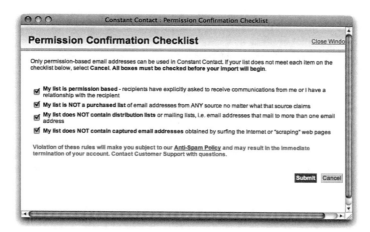

Figure 16.10

Agree to the upload terms.

6. Now you need to map the data that you have uploaded to the Constant Contact fields. The interface is different from that of Vertical Response, but the object is the same, as you can see in Figure 16.11.

Figure 16.11

Match uploaded data to bulk database fields.

7. Your import begins, as shown in Figure 16.12.

Figure 16.12
Start the import.

8. When the import is done, you can check the results, as shown in Figure 16.13. Just as with Vertical Response, check for errors in the upload.

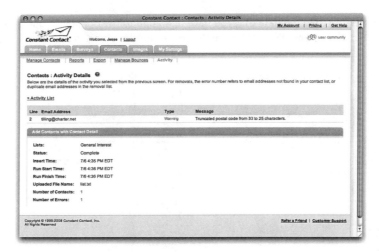

Figure 16.13
Check the upload results.

Downloading Bulk Email Data to Bento

Downloads operate in much the same way as uploads; the difference is that Constant Contact downloads a file, whereas Vertical Response displays the downloaded data in a window from which you can copy it to a document on your computer.

DOWNLOADING DATA WITH VERTICAL RESPONSE

The download process for Vertical Response is pretty much the reverse of the upload process:

1. From the Mailing Lists screen, as shown previously in Figure 16.1, choose Download from the Action link by the list you want to download.

In the next screen (shown in Figure 16.14), choose to download the file. (CSV is easiest and is necessary for Bento 1.) You can choose to limit the download to unsubscribes and/or bounces; this option can help you update Bento library records that you may want to mark with this information.

2. Finally, choose the bulk email database fields to download.

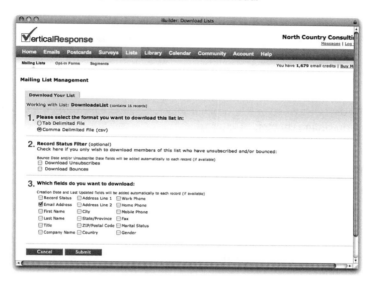

Figure 16.14

Configure the download.

3. When the list is ready, you can choose to download it, as shown in Figure 16.15.

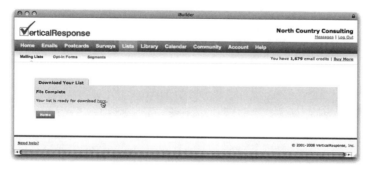

Figure 16.15

Download the data.

4. Choosing to download the list displays the data in your browser window. Copy it and paste it into a blank document. A TextEdit document is a good choice; TextEdit comes with Mac OS X. Just remember to choose Format > Make Plain Text so that the document is saved as a text document. Figure 16.16 shows the downloaded and pasted data in a TextEdit window.

Figure 16.16

Paste the data into a TextEdit document.

5. Save the TextEdit document and import it into Bento as a CSV file using the procedures outlined in the preceding chapter.

DOWNLOADING DATA WITH CONSTANT CONTACT

Finally, the download process for Constant Contact follows:

1. To download data with Constant Contact, start from the same screen shown previously in Figure 16.6, but this time choose Export Data. You see the window shown in Figure 16.17 where you can select the data to download. Because the structure of Constant Contact databases is different from that of Vertical Response, you can choose the types of information to download, as shown in Figure 16.17.

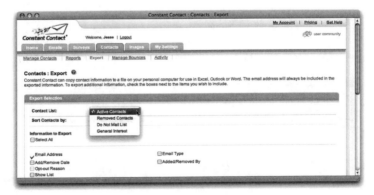

Figure 16.17

Choose the data to download.

2. If you are using your own modification date, you download the Add/Remove date for that field. Also, to download your entire list (including the removes), you need to do two downloads.

The downloadable data continues further down the window, as shown in Figure 16.18.

Figure 16.18

Check all the fields you want to download.

Constant Contact downloads the file. (You do not have to copy data and paste it into TextEdit.) After the file has been downloaded, simply import it into Bento.

17

Bento Quickies

Introducing Bento Quickies

As noted in the Introduction, organizing five items makes them more useful than hundreds or thousands of unorganized items. This chapter provides you with some suggestions for Bento Quickies—simple libraries that you can put together in minutes (or even seconds) to make your life easier and more organized. You can use them as-is, or as jumping-off points for your own libraries. Because they are so simple, you may decide to use them to implement related records in other solutions. Adding related records to a Bento library is often the fastest and easiest way to expand its functionality with minimum added complexity.

One point that you will notice is that there are organization tools built into Bento that you do not have to worry about. Just by deciding that you will create a Bento library to track something (serial numbers of software, car maintenance appointments, or whatever), you have already provided the first type of organization: a place to store a certain kind of data. After you have done that, Bento steps in by automatically providing you with creation and modification dates. From there, you are on your own. However, with this structure (the information to be organized and the creation/modification dates), just entering a single data value can provide useful results.

IN THIS CHAPTER

- Introducing Bento Quickies   225
- Nexts   226
- Software Inventory   227
- Clippings   229
- Nos   229
- Jokes   230
- Recipes   230
- Shopping Sources   231
- Fashion Parade   231
- Gift List   232

> ## NOTE
>
> For more Bento Quickies, see this book's web page at www.thebentobook.com. And if you have ideas for your own Bento Quickies, feel free to add them there.

Nexts

Bento's integration with iCal makes it easy to track events and tasks. But sometimes you need to schedule events in the future before you have an actual date. Nexts lets you do that.

For example, if you take your car in for an oil change, you may want to remember to bring it in again three months later. You do not want to make an appointment yet, but you do want to remember. Figure 17.1 shows a simple Nexts Bento Quickie.

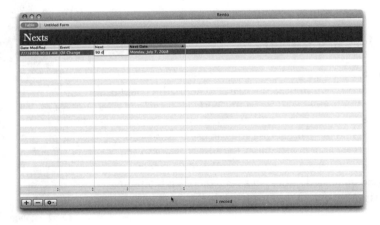

Figure 17.1

Use Nexts to keep track of upcoming not-yet-scheduled events.

Use Nexts to track all the upcoming events that you need to schedule from oil changes to doctors' appointments—anything with an approximate date and no actual event scheduled.

You can take advantage of Bento's built-in Date Modified field to use as a starting date. Then create a field called Event that describes what it is that you are tracking. A duration field called Next lets you enter the amount of time before the next event. Finally, a calculation field called Next Date adds Next to Date Modified to tell you when the next event will be.

Figure 17.1 shows one thing to watch out for when you're using duration fields. You can enter days (d), hours (h), minutes (m), or weeks (w) but there is no months component to a duration field. (Perhaps because months (m) would conflict with minutes (m).) If you need to enter three months, instead enter 90 days, as shown in Figure 17.1. You can also enter seconds (s) in a duration field, but chances are a timeframe that short is too short for you to use Bento to track it.

As soon as you create a new record, the Next field is blank, and Next Date is calculated from that. Then enter the new duration in Next, as shown in Figure 17.1. As soon as you leave the field, Bento converts 90 days (or whatever you have entered) to a standard duration field, as shown in Figure 17.2.

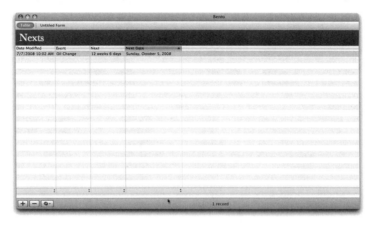

Figure 17.2
Bento converts duration fields and calculates the Next Date.

Although Bento creates a default form for each library you create, you can work with Nexts simply in the table view. Remember that you can sort columns easily to see upcoming events that need to be scheduled with actual dates. If you want, you can add a new field called Actual Date in which you can type a date (and, perhaps, time) for the actual date you have set for the projected Next Date event.

> **NOTE**
>
> Working from the automatically created modification date means you do not have to manually enter a starting date. Even though the date of the oil change might not exactly be the modification date (it might have been yesterday or the day before), the simplicity probably outweighs the slight lack of precision. And if you are considering durations of weeks or months, the exact date does not matter. If it does, create a specific starting field. Also, note that by using the modification date, you can automatically update the record for the next oil change, just by making a modification to it. For example, if you entered "25,000 mile oil change," you could change 25,000 to 35,000 to change the modification date, and the Next Date field would be updated properly.

Software Inventory

In many cases, you need a software serial number (or license number) to install or upgrade software. Sometimes, this number is on a sticker attached to the packaging of the software. Many people have a shelf of software boxes that they keep in large part so that they know where the serial numbers are.

With the advent of online delivery of software, the serial numbers or license numbers are often delivered in a confirmation email. Some people set up a special folder in Mail to keep these messages.

You can set up a Bento Quickie to keep track of software serial numbers. Whenever you get a new piece of software, enter a new record with the name and version number of the software; then enter the serial number, as shown in Figure 17.3.

Figure 17.3

Keep track of software with a Bento Quickie.

You can use the software inventory to keep track of all your software—even the software that does not require license or serial numbers. You can add expiration date fields for licenses, and you can use the modification date as in Nexts to keep track of when a record was last changed. (Just add the built-in Modification Date field to the form.)

TIP

If you have been moving from Mac to Mac over the years, you may have used the Migration Assistant and a FireWire cable to move your files and applications from one computer to the next one. This technique makes the transition simple. However, it may mean that you do not know what applications you have on your hard disk today. If there were a catastrophic crash (or if your computer were stolen), could you restore the software? Having the serial numbers is one thing, but simply knowing what you had is another. Take an afternoon to enter all the names of the software in your Applications folder into a Bento Software Inventory (and then back up the Bento database). Then keep up to date in the future as you add new software.

 In Bento 2, you can even create a link to an email message that contains the serial number, but you have to remember not to delete the message.

Clippings

Create a Bento Quickie to keep track of clippings from books, newspapers, or websites. Copy and paste text into a Bento Quickie and add the citation. Add quotes or comments from commentators, comedians, experts, or friends. If you're trying to put together a paper, report, letter, or other document, you can go to your Clippings Bento Quickie to find out exactly where you found the clipping or quote.

Authors and other people spend a lot of time tracking down the source of quotes that they remember but for which they cannot remember the source. A Clippings Bento Quickie will solve that problem for you, as shown in Figure 17.4.

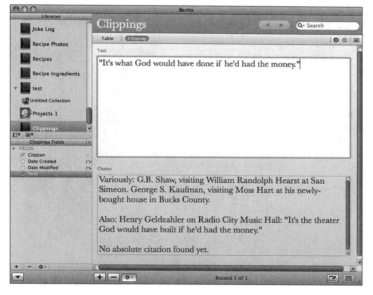

Figure 17.4

Keep track of clippings.

Nos

Do you invite people to parties? Ask people to volunteer? Solicit contributions for worthy causes? If so, you can easily add a field to the Bento Address Book to indicate that someone would prefer not to be asked, but not everyone you might talk to is in your Address Book. When you are working on a project or using a mailing list, you can also indicate who does not want to participate. But what about people who would prefer not to be contacted for anything? Create a Nos Bento Quickie listing people who would not like to be contacted in this way. You don't need names ("man in gray house on corner" is fine). Bento lets you organize lots of complex data in many ways, but sometimes the most value comes from organizing just a single piece of data. Your Nos library can contain a single field—Who—which can be a name or description. That, together with the name of the library (Nos), tells you all you need to know.

Jokes

Use a Bento Quickie to keep track of jokes you hear and tell. Figure 17.5 shows one way of doing this. There's space for you to type in the joke, and you can add video of the joke as it is told. If you are a stand-up comic or aspire to be one, keep a log of where and when you have used the joke and what the reaction was. The joke log is a related records field that has just those three fields in it.

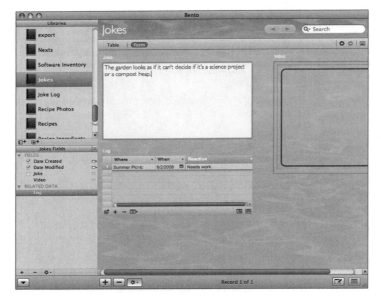

Figure 17.5

Keep track of jokes.

Recipes

From the dawn of the age of personal computing, keeping track of recipes is a task that has been proposed as an ideal candidate for a home computer. With a Bento Quickie, you can do much more than just store your recipes. Figure 17.6 shows a Recipe Bento Quickie.

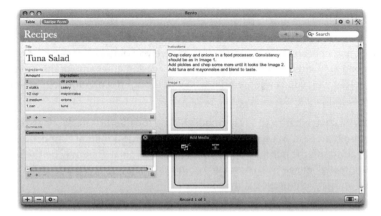

Figure 17.6

Organize recipes with your comments and images.

This library has two sets of related records: comments and ingredients. In addition, there is space for two images. (You can obviously create more if you want.) Even if this is your recipe and it is just for your own reference, reminding yourself what the recipe should look like at various points is helpful. Even more so can be an image of the bowl, pot, or serving dish that you have learned is just the right size to serve your masterpiece.

Shopping Sources

You probably do not have much trouble figuring out where to buy milk or a garden hose. If you need something that is hard to find, the Internet is the place to look. But what about hard-to-find items that you do not need very often and that are not worth the cost of shipping from the Internet? Make a Bento Quickie library for Shopping Sources. You can make do with two fields: what and where. Identify what the object or service is, and then type in where you found it. This approach works well for infrequently purchased small items such as the replacement battery for a doorbell or a light bulb that fits a special fixture. Once every few years, you need to replace them, and knowing which store you finally found them in the last time can be a timesaver.

Fashion Parade

Do you make custom items such as scarves, sweaters, even dog coats? Customers often like to show you how they (or their pets) look in your creation, so encourage them to send you a photo. Add the photo to a Bento Quickie along with fields such as the person's name and contact information, what he or she paid, and a checkbox to let you know whether you can use the image in your marketing. As with so many Bento projects, having the organization structure in place lets you collect data as you go along. When it is time to put together a mailing, web page, or catalog, it is too late to scrounge around for photos.

Gift List

If friends, relatives, and colleagues are kind enough to give you gifts, keep track of them in a Bento Quickie. All you need are fields for the item, the date or occasion, the name of the giver, and perhaps a note or comment. That way, you can remember who was thoughtful enough to give you the tea cozy in the shape of a bagpipe.

Keeping track of who gave what to you is a thoughtful use for a Bento Quickie. It also is helpful if you have occasion to regift an item. Many people find that they forge a mental connection between the giver and the gift, although the connection is somewhat subliminal. That may be the reason why regifting to the original giver seems to be a fairly common occurrence. A Bento Quickie Gift List will solve the problem and prevent unpleasantness.

NOTE

If you happen to be the person who, in pre-Bento days, gave a tea cozy in the shape of a bag-pipe to this author, please accept my apologies.

Index

A

access to personal databases, 9-10

acounts, creating, 11

Activity field (Garden/Nature log), 170

Add Field command (Card menu), 116

Address Book
 Address Book library
  adding fields to, 116-118
  adding forms to, 116
  Bento/Address Book integration, 115-116
  creating, 113
  example, 114-115
 contacts, sharing with MobileMe, 148-150
 limitations of, 8
 related record fields, implementing, 196
 synchronizing
  definition of, 118
  with iPhone, 121-123
  with MobileMe, 118-120

with MobileMe push technology, 124
with PDAs, 123
updating with data detectors, 124-125
working with, 142-146

Address Book and iCal Setup command (File menu), 13

Address Book library. See also Address Book
 adding fields to, 116-118
 adding forms to, 116
 Bento/Address Book integration, 115-116
 creating, 113
 example, 114-115

address fields
 adding to forms, 72-73
 in Bento 1, 69-70
 in Bento 2, 70-72
 overview, 69

Advanced Find, 31-33

Amount field (Garden/Nature log), 170

analyzing Garden/Nature log database, 173-175

ARPAnet, 208

as-of dates, 168

automatic counter fields, 16, 89

automatic login, 10

B

backing up hard disk, importance of, 123

Bento 1 compared to Bento 2, 1-3

Bento discussion forum, 6

Bento menu commands, Preferences, 40

Bento preferences, setting, 40

Bento Quickies
 Clippings, 229
 Fashion Parade, 231
 Gift List, 232
 Jokes, 230
 Nexts, 226-227
 Nos, 229-230
 overview, 225
 Recipes, 230-231
 Shopping Sources, 231
 Software Inventory, 227-228

Bento window

controlling which sections
are displayed, 22-23

Fields list, 22, 37-38

overview, 21-22

Records area, 22

creating records, 27

deleting records, 33

entering text data, 27-28

finding data, 29-33

overview, 24-26

printing records, 28-29

Source list, 22, 37

**bidirectional
relationships, 191**

bulk email (spam)

CAN-SPAM act, 210-211

downloading bulk email
data to Bento

with Constant Contact,
222-223

with Vertical Response,
220-222

ISP rules, 210

mail filters, 209-210

overview, 208-209

sending via vendors,
211-212

uploading bulk email data
from Bento, 213-214

with Constant Contact,
217-220

with Vertical Response,
214-216

C

Calculation dialog, 82-83

calculation fields, 17

Calculation dialog, 82-83

Calories Burned field, 86

Duration field, 84-85

overview, 82

**calendar data (iCal),
managing, 130, 135-137.**
See also iCal

Calendar list (iCal), 128

**Calories Rate field (Exercise
Log), 81-82**

CAN-SPAM act, 210-211

capabilities of Bento, 8-9

**Card menu commands, Add
Field, 116**

cardinality, 178

changing field types, 14

checkbox fields, 16, 88-89

checking spelling, 27

choice fields, 16, 87

Classes template

table view, 43-44

form view, 45-46

**cleaning up imported data,
62-63**

Clippings Bento Quickie, 229

**clippings, organizing into
Bento Quickie, 229**

collections

adding records to, 108

creating empty
collections, 108

creating from selected
records, 109

definition, 18, 107

example, 107

overview, 18-19

Smart Collections, 19-20,
109-111, 173-175

columns, 190

**command-separated-values
(CSV) data, importing,
57-62**

commands

Bento menu, Preferences, 40

Card menu, Add Field, 116

Edit menu, Delete
Library, 24

File menu

Address Book and iCal
Setup, 13

Export, 206

Import, 23, 58

New Collection, 108

New Library, 23, 154

New Smart
Collection, 109

Print, 28

Format menu, Themes, 48

Forms menu

Duplicate Form, 46

Rename Form, 46

Insert menu

Current Date and
Time, 27

Delete Field, 38

Duplicate Field, 38

Duplicate Form, 180

New Field, 38, 156

Records menu

Advanced Find, 31-33

Delete Selected
Record(s), 33

Duplicate Record, 27

New Record, 27

Edit menu, Spelling, 27

View menu, Customize
Form, 48

**communicating with multi-
ple people, 208**

**complexity, managing with
Bento, 189-191**

**computers, definition
for MobileMe
synchronization, 120**

configuring Bento
preferences, 40

Constant Contact
downloading bulk email
data to Bento, 222-223
uploading data from Bento,
217-220

contacts (Address Book),
sharing with MobileMe,
148-150

Contacts library
address fields
adding to forms, 72-73
in Bento 1, 69-70
in Bento 2, 70-72
overview, 69
creating, 66-67
lists
adding to forms, 72-73
in Bento 1, 69-70
in Bento 2, 70-72
overview, 69
overview, 65-66
views, 67-69

converting
between events and To Do
items (iCal), 130
field types, 14

counters, automatic, 16, 89

Crops database, 170-171

Crops field (Garden/Nature
log), 170

CSV (command-
separated-values) data,
importing, 57-62

currency fields, 16

Current Date and Time
command (Insert menu), 27

Customize Form command
(View menu), 48

customizing
fields, 148
forms, 148
fields, 48-50
themes, 47
Projects library, 153

D

data, finding
with Advanced Find, 31-33
with search field, 29-31

data detectors
with iCal, 134-135
updating Address Book
with, 124-125

data entry
addresses
adding to forms, 72-73
in Bento 1, 69-70
in Bento 2, 70-72
overview, 69
automatic counters, 89
calculations
Calculation dialog, 82-83
Calories Burned field, 86
Duration field, 84-85
overview, 82
checkbox values, 88
choice values, 87
currency values, 89
customizing fields, 148
dates
date and time field
controls, 79-80
Start Date field (Exercise
Log), 79
Stop Date field (Exercise
Log), 77-78
editing fields, 90-92
file list fields, 17, 181-183
form fields. *See* forms

importing data
into existing libraries,
200-204
overview, 199
legacy data
in Bento 2, 63
cleaning up imported
data, 62-63
CSV (command-
separated-values)
data, 57-62
data formats, 54-56
overview, 53-54
lists. *See* lists
media fields, 16
message list fields, 17
numbers, 81-82
ratings, 90
related records list fields
adding data to, 103-105
adding to forms, 100
formatting, 101-102
restrictions on, 105-106
reviewing related
records, 103-104
summarizing, 103
storyboards
Image field, 193
Length field, 193
Notes field, 193
Place field, 193
related record fields,
195-196
Script field, 193
Sequence field, 193
Setting field, 193
Status field, 193
Time field, 193
Title field, 193
text data, 27-28
times, 79-80

data, exporting
exporting files from libraries, 205-206
exporting libraries as templates, 206

data formats, importing, 54-56

data, importing
in Bento 2, 63
cleaning up imported data, 62-63
CSV (command-separated-values) data, 57-62
data formats, 54-56
importing libraries as templates, 206
into existing libraries, 200-204
overview, 53-54, 199

data structure (iCal), 132

databases. *See* **personal databases**

date and time field controls, 79-80

Date field (Garden/Nature log), 170

date fields, 16
as-of dates, 168
date and time field controls, 79-80
entering current dates, 27
Garden/Nature log, 168
Start Date field (Exercise Log), 79
Stop Date field (Exercise Log), 77-78

Delete Field command (Insert menu), 38

Delete Library command (Edit menu), 24

Delete Selected Record(s) command (Records menu), 33

deleting
fields in Bento 1, 38
libraries, 24
records, 33

Details layout (Projects template), 141

dialogs
Calculation, 82-83
Home, 11
New Library, 23, 67
Preferences, 12
Reset Synchronization Data, 120-121
Theme Chooser, 47

displaying event details, 131

do-not-contact list, organizing into Bento Quickie, 229-230

downloadable files, 6

downloading
Bento, 11
bulk email data from Bento with Constant Contact, 222-223
with Vertical Response, 220-222

Duplicate Field command (Insert menu), 38

Duplicate Form command
Forms menu, 46
Insert menu, 180

Duplicate Record command (Records menu), 27

duplicating
fields in Bento 1, 38
forms, 46

duration fields, 16, 84-86

E

ease of use (Bento), 9

Edit menu commands
Delete Library, 24
Spelling, 27

editing
events, 131
fields, 36, 90-92

email lists
bulk email (spam)
CAN-SPAM act, 210-211
downloading bulk email data to Bento, 220-223
ISP rules, 210
overview, 208-209
sending via vendors, 211-212
uploading bulk email data from Bento, 213-220
email lists, 207
mail filters, 209-210
Mail records, working with, 146-147

events (iCal)
converting to To Dos, 130
displaying event details, 131
editing, 131
sharing with MobileMe, 148-150
synchronizing, 137

Exercise Log library
automatic counter fields, 89
Calories Rate field, 81-82
checkbox fields, 88
choice fields, 87
currency fields, 89
date and time field controls, 79-80
Duration field, 84-86
overview, 75-77

rating fields, 90
Start Date field, 79
Stop Date field, 77-78
Export command (File menu), 206
exporting data
exporting files from libraries, 205-206
exporting libraries as templates, 206

F

Fashion Parade Bento Quickie, 231
fields
adding to Address Book library, 116-118
address fields
adding to forms, 72-73
in Bento 1, 69-70
in Bento 2, 70-72
overview, 69
automatic counter fields, 16, 89
calculation fields, 17
Calculation dialog, 82-83
Calories Burned field, 86
Duration field, 84-85
overview, 82
changing type of, 14
checkbox fields, 16, 88
choice fields, 16, 87
creating, 38
currency fields, 16, 89
customizing, 148
date fields, 16
date and time field controls, 79-80
Start Date field (Exercise Log), 79
Stop Date field (Exercise Log), 77-78

definition, 13
deleting, 38
duplicating, 38
duration fields, 16
editing, 90-92
Exercise Log fields
Calories Rate field, 81-82
date and time field controls, 79-80
Start Date, 79
Stop Date, 77-78
file list fields, 17
adding to group projects, 181-183
form fields, customizing, 48-50
formatting, 14
Garden/Nature log fields
Activity field, 170
Amount field, 170
Crops field, 170
Date field, 170
date fields, 168
high/low temperature fields, 168
Highlights of the Day field, 169
media fields, 169
Notes field, 170
media fields, 16
message list fields, 17
names, 14
Notes field (Project Notes library), 156
number fields, 16
Calories Rate field, 81-82
creating and formatting, 81-82
rating fields, 16, 90
related records list fields, 17
adding data to, 103
adding to forms, 100
formatting, 101-105

restrictions on, 105-106
reviewing related records, 103-104
summarizing, 103
removing, 148
renaming, 38, 148
storyboard fields
Image, 193
Length, 193
Notes, 193
Place, 193
related record fields, 195-196
Script, 193
Sequence, 193
Setting, 193
Status, 193
Time, 193
Title, 193
text fields, 16
time fields, 16, 79-80
Fields list (Bento window), 22, 37-38
file list fields, 17
adding to group projects, 181-183
File menu commands
Address Book and iCal Setup, 13
Export, 206
Import, 23, 58
New Collection, 108
New Library, 23, 154
New Smart Collection, 109
Print, 28
FileMaker, 6-7
files
downloadable files, 6
organizing, 183-184
filters, mail, 209-210

finding data
with Advanced Find, 31-33
with search field, 29-31

folders, Library/Application Support/Bento, 13

form view of Classes template, 45-46

Format menu commands, Themes, 48

formatting
automatic counter fields, 89
checkbox fields, 88
choice fields, 87
currency fields, 89
fields, 14
number fields, 81-82
rating fields, 90
related records list fields, 101-102

forms
adding to Address Book library, 116
address fields, adding, 72-73
creating for group projects, 180-181
dragging related libraries onto, 98-99
duplicating, 46
fields, customizing, 48-50
horizontal separators, 50
lists, adding, 72-73
overview, 43
renaming, 46
revising, 148
spacers, 50
themes, 47
tools, 51-52

Forms menu commands
Duplicate Form, 46
Rename Form, 46

formulas. *See* **calculation fields**

G

Garden/Nature log
analyzing database, 173-175
creating basic library, 167-170
creating related libraries, 170-172
planning, 165-167
Smart Collections, 173-175

Gift List Bento Quickie, 232

group projects
Many People = Many Projects structure, 187
One Person = Many Projects structure, 184-185
One Person = One Project structure
file list fields, 181-183
file organization, 183-184
form creation, 180-181
overview, 179-180
One Project = Many People structure, 186
organizing, 178
planning, 177-178

H

hard disk backups, importance of, 123

Highlights of the Day field (Garden/Nature log), 169

history of storyboards, 192

Home dialog, 11

horizontal separators, 50

I

iCal, 142-146
Bento iCal libraries, 132-134
Calendar list, 128
calendars, 130
data structure, 132
events
converting to To Dos, 130
displaying event details, 131
editing, 131
sharing with MobileMe, 148-150
Mail data detectors with, 134-135
managing calendar data, 135-137
overview, 127
related record fields, implementing, 196
Search Results pane, 128-130
synchronizing iCal events, 137
To Dos, 128
converting to events, 130
displaying event details, 131
editing, 131

.ics files, 132

Image field (storyboards), 193

Import command (File menu), 23, 58

importing data
importing libraries as templates, 206
into existing libraries, 200-204

legacy data
- in Bento 2, 63
- cleaning up imported data, 62-63
- CSV (command-separated-values) data, 57-62
- data formats, 54-56
- overview, 53-54
- overview, 199

Ins & Outs library
- creating, 96-98
- dragging onto Inventory library form, 99
- relating to Inventory library, 98-99

Insert menu commands
- Current Date and Time, 27
- Delete Field, 38
- Duplicate Field, 38
- Duplicate Form, 180
- New Field, 38, 156

Internet Service Providers (ISPs), bulk email rules, 210

inventory
- Inventory library
  - overview, 93-96
  - tracking inventory with relationships, 98-105
- Software Inventory Bento Quickie, 227-228

Inventory library
- overview, 93-96
- tracking inventory with relationships, 98
  - adding data to related records list field, 103-105
  - adding related records list field, 100

dragging related libraries onto forms, 98-99
- formatting related records list field, 101-102
- restrictions on related records list field, 105-106
- reviewing related records, 103-104
- summarizing related records list field, 103

iPhone, synchronizing Address Book with, 121-123

ISPs (Internet Service Providers), bulk email rules, 210

iTunes, limitations of, 8

J-K-L

Jokes Bento Quickie, 230

jokes, organizing into Bento Quickie, 230

layouts, 191

legacy data, importing into Bento
- in Bento 2, 63
- cleaning up imported data, 62-63
- CSV (command-separated-values) data, 57-62
- data formats, 54-56
- overview, 53-54

legislation, CAN-SPAM act, 210-211

Length field (storyboards), 193

libraries
- Address Book library
  - adding fields to, 116-118
  - adding forms to, 116
  - Bento/Address Book integration, 115-116
  - creating, 113
  - example, 114-115
- Contacts library
  - address fields, 69-73
  - creating, 66-67
  - lists, 69-73
  - overview, 65-66
  - views, 67-69
- creating, 23, 154-155
  - from Projects template, 140-141
  - from scratch, 96-98
- definition, 18
- deleting, 24
- email libraries
  - downloading bulk email data to Bento, 220-223
  - uploading bulk email data from Bento, 213-220
- Exercise Log
  - automatic counter fields, 89
  - Calories Burned field, 86
  - Calories Rate field, 81-82
  - checkbox fields, 88
  - choice fields, 87
  - currency fields, 89
  - date and time field controls, 79-80
  - Duration field, 84-85
  - overview, 75-77
  - rating fields, 90
  - Start Date field, 79
  - Stop Date field, 77-78
- exporting as templates, 206
- exporting data from, 205-206

Garden/Nature log libraries
  analyzing database,
    173-175
  basic library, creating,
    167-170
  related libraries, creating,
    170-172
  Smart Collections,
    173-175
iCal libraries, 132-134
importing as templates, 206
importing data into, 23,
  200-204
Ins & Outs
  creating, 96-98
  dragging onto Inventory
    library form, 99
  relating to Inventory
    library, 98-99
Inventory
  overview, 93-96
  tracking inventory with
    relationships, 98-106
naming, 23
Project Notes library
  adding list of related
    records to, 157-160
  creating new library,
    154-155
  creating Notes field, 156
  overview, 154
  relationships, 161-164
Projects library, 139-141
  in Bento 1, 151-152
  in Bento 2, 152
  customizing, 153
  overview, 151
storyboard
  libraries, creating
    Image field, 193
    Length field, 193
    Notes field, 193

overview, 192-193
Place field, 193
related record fields,
  195-196
Script field, 193
Sequence field, 193
Setting field, 193
Status field, 193
Time field, 193
Title field, 193

Libraries & Fields pane, 39-40

**Library/Application
  Support/Bento folder, 13**

lists
  adding to forms, 72-73
  in Bento 1, 69-70
  in Bento 2, 70-72
  Calendar list (iCal), 128
  email lists
    bulk email (spam),
      208-212
    downloading bulk email
      data to Bento, 220-223
    mail filters, 209-210
    overview, 207
    uploading bulk email
      data from Bento,
      213-220
  Gift List Bento Quickie, 232
  overview, 69
  To Dos list (iCal), 128
    converting to
      events, 130

login options, 10

logs, Garden/Nature
  analyzing database, 173-175
  creating basic library,
    167-170
  creating related libraries,
    170-172
  planning, 165-167
  Smart Collections, 173-175

M

Mail data detectors
  with iCal, 134-135
  updating Address Book
    with, 124-125

**Mail records, working with,
  146-147**

mailing lists. *See* email lists

**managing calendar data
  (iCal), 135-137**

**Many People = Many
  Projects structure (group
  projects), 187**

**many-to-many
  relationship, 178**

Mati, Jose, 192

media fields, 16, 169

message list fields, 17

**MobileMe synchronization,
  118-120, 124, 148-150**

moving form fields, 48

N

naming
  fields, 14
  libraries, 23

**Nature log. *See*
  Garden/Nature log**

navigating Bento window
  controlling which sections
    are displayed, 22-23
  Fields list, 22, 37-38
  overview, 21-22
  Records area, 22
    creating records, 27
    deleting records, 33
    entering text data, 27-28
    finding data, 29, 31-33

overview, 24-26
printing records, 28-29
Source list, 22, 37

need for Bento, 8

New Collection command (File menu), 108

New Field command (Insert menu), 38, 156

New Library command (File menu), 23, 154

New Library dialog, 23, 67

New Record command (Records menu), 27

New Smart Collection command (File menu), 109

Nexts Bento Quickie, 226-227

Nos Bento Quickie, 229-230

notes, Project Notes library
adding list of related records to, 157-160
creating new library, 154-155
creating Notes field, 156
overview, 154
relationships, 161-164

Notes fields
Garden/Nature log, 170
Project Notes library, 156
storyboards, 193

number fields, 16, 81-82

O

obtaining Bento, 11

One Person = Many Projects structure (group projects), 184-185

One Person = One Project structure (group projects)
file list fields, 181-183
file organization, 183-184
form creating, 180-181
overview, 179-180

One Project = Many People structure (group projects), 186

one-to-many relationship, 178

one-to-one relationship, 178, 191

organizing. *See also* **Bento Quickies**
files, 183-184
group projects, 178

Overview form (Projects template), 140

P

panes, Libraries & Fields, 39-40

pasting data into table views, 36-37

PDAs (Personal Digital Assistants), synchronizing Address Book with, 123

personal databases
access to, 9-10
capabilities of, 8-9
collections
definition, 18
overview, 18-19
Smart Collections, 19-20
Crops, 170-171
ease of use, 9
fields. *See* fields
libraries. *See* libraries
need for, 8
records. *See* records

Place field (storyboards), 193

planning
Garden/Nature log, 165-167
group projects, 177-178
storyboards, 189-191

preferences, setting, 40

Preferences command (Bento menu), 40

Preferences dialog, 12

Print command (File menu), 28

printing records, 28-29

procedural programming, 9

programming, 9

Project Notes library
adding list of related records to, 157-160
creating new library, 154-155
creating Notes field, 156
overview, 154
relationships, 161-164

Projects library, 139-141
in Bento 1, 151-152
in Bento 2, 152
customizing, 153
overview, 151

pull technology, 208

push technology, 124, 208

Q

queries (SQL), 190

Quickies
Clippings, 229
Fashion Parade, 231
Gift List, 232
Jokes, 230
Nexts, 226-227
Nos, 229-230

overview, 225
Recipes, 230-231
Shopping Sources, 231
Software Inventory, 227-228

R

rating fields, 16, 90

Recipes Bento Quickie, 230-231

recipes, organizing into Bento Quickie, 230-231

record fields (storyboards), 195-196

Record menu commands, Advanced Find, 31-33

records
adding to collections, 108
adding to Project Notes
library, 157-160
Address Book records,
142-146
collections
adding records to, 108
creating empty
collections, 108
creating from selected
records, 109
definition of, 107
example, 107
Smart Collections,
109-111
creating, 27
creating collections
from, 109
definition, 17-18
deleting, 33
entering data into. *See*
data entry
iCal records, 142-146

Mail records, 146-147
printing, 28-29
related records
Address Book records,
142-146
iCal records, 142-146
Mail records, 146-147
related records list fields,
100-106
related records, reviewing,
103-104
table views
in Bento 1, 33-35
in Bento 2, 35-37
editing fields with
(Bento 2), 36
pasting data into in
(Bento 2), 36-37
sorting (Bento 2), 36

Records area (Bento window), 22
creating records, 27
deleting records, 33
entering text data, 27-28
finding data
with Advanced Find,
31-33
with search field, 29-31
overview, 24-26
printing records, 28-29

Records menu commands
Delete Selected
Record(s), 33
Duplicate Record, 27
New Record, 27

related records
adding to Project Notes
library, 157-160
Address Book records,
142-146
iCal records, 142-146
Mail records, 146-147

related records list fields, 17
adding data to, 103-105
adding to forms, 100
formatting, 101-102
restrictions on, 105-106
reviewing related
records, 103-104
summarizing, 103
reviewing, 103-104

related records list fields, 17
adding data to, 103-105
adding to forms, 100
formatting, 101-102
restrictions on, 105-106
reviewing related records,
103-104
summarizing, 103

relational databases, 190

relationships
bidirectional
relationships, 191
creating
adding data to
related records list
field, 103-105
adding related records
list field, 100
by dragging related
libraries onto
forms, 98-99
formatting related
records list field,
101-102
restrictions on
related records list
field, 105-106
summarizing related
records list field, 103
definition, 190
many-to-many
relationship, 178
one-to-many
relationship, 178

one-to-one relationship, 178, 191
in Project Notes library, 161-164
reviewing related records, 103-104
tracking inventory with
adding data to related records list field, 103-105
adding related records list field, 100
dragging related libraries onto forms, 98-99
formatting related records list field, 101-102
restrictions on related records list field, 105-106
reviewing related records, 103-104
summarizing related records list field, 103
unidirectional relationships, 191

removing. *See* deleting

Rename Form command (Forms menu), 46

renaming
fields, 38, 148
forms, 46

Reset Synchronization Data dialog, 120-121

resizing form fields, 48

reviewing related records, 103-104

revising forms, 148

roles of Bento, 8-9

rows, 190

S

Script field (storyboards), 193

Search Results pane (iCal), 128-130

sending bulk email via vendors, 211-212

Sequence field (storyboards), 193

setting Bento preferences, 40

Setting field (storyboards), 193

sharing
Address Book contacts with MobileMe, 148-150
iCal events with MobileMe, 148-150

Shopping Sources Bento Quickie, 231

shopping sources, organizing into Bento Quickie, 231

single-value fields in storyboards, 193-194

Smart Collections, 19-20, 109-111, 173-175

Software Inventory Bento Quickie, 227-228

sorting table views, 36

Source list (Bento window), 22, 37

spacers, 50

spam
CAN-SPAM act, 210-211
downloading bulk email data to Bento
with Constant Contact, 222-223
with Vertical Response, 220-222

ISP rules, 210
mail filters, 209-210
overview, 208-209
sending via vendors, 211-212
uploading bulk email data from Bento, 213-214
with Constant Contact, 217-220
with Vertical Response, 214, 216

spell check, 27

Spelling command (Edit menu), 27

Spotlight, 183

spreadsheets, importing, 63

SQL, 190

Start Date field (Exercise Log), 79

Status field (storyboards), 193

Stop Date field (Exercise Log), 77-78

storyboards
history of, 192
planning, 189-191
storyboard libraries, creating
Image field, 193
Length field, 193
Notes field, 193
overview, 192-193
Place field, 193
related record fields, 195-196
Script field, 193
Sequence field, 193
Setting field, 193
Status field, 193
Time field, 193
Title field, 193
suitability of Bento for, 192

summarizing related records list fields, 103

synchronizing
Address Book, 118
with iPhone, 121-123
with MobileMe
with MobileMe push
technology, 124
with PDAs, 123
definition of, 118
iCal events, 137
MobileMe synchronization,
118-120, 124, 148-150

T

table views
of Classes template, 43-44
editing fields with
(Bento 2), 36
in Bento 1, 33-35
in Bento 2, 35-36
editing fields with table
views, 36
pasting data into table
views, 36-37
sorting table views, 36
pasting data into
(Bento 2), 36-37
sorting (Bento 2), 36

tables, 190

**temperature fields
(Garden/Nature log), 168**

templates
Classes template
form view, 45-46
table view, 43-44
exporting libraries as, 206
importing libraries as, 206

**text data, entering into
records, 27-28**

text fields, 16

Theme Chooser dialog, 47

themes, adding to forms, 47

**Themes command (Format
menu), 48**

time fields, 16
date and time field controls,
79-80
entering current time, 27
storyboards, 193

Time Machine, 123

Title field (storyboards), 193

To Dos (iCal), 128
converting to events, 130

tools, Form tools, 51-52

**tracking inventory
with relationships**
adding data to related
records list field, 103-105
adding related records list
field, 100
dragging related libraries
onto forms, 98-99
formatting related records
list field, 101-102
restrictions on records list
field, 105-106
reviewing related records,
103-104
summarizing related
records list field, 103

types (fields)
changing, 14
definition, 13

U

**unidirectional
relationships, 191**

unsolicited bulk email. *See*
bulk email

**updating Address Book with
data detectors, 124-125**

**uploading bulk email data
from Bento, 213-214**
with Constant Contact,
217-220
with Vertical Response,
214-216

V-W-X-Y-Z

**vendors, sending bulk email
with, 211-212**

verifying imported data, 62

Vertical Response
downloading bulk email
data to Bento, 220-222
uploading data from Bento,
214-216

**View menu commands,
Customize Form, 48**

views
form view, 45-46
table views
of Classes template,
43-44
editing fields with
(Bento 2), 36
in Bento 1, 33-35
in Bento 2, 35-37
pasting data into (Bento
2), 36-37
sorting (Bento 2), 36

web sites, 6

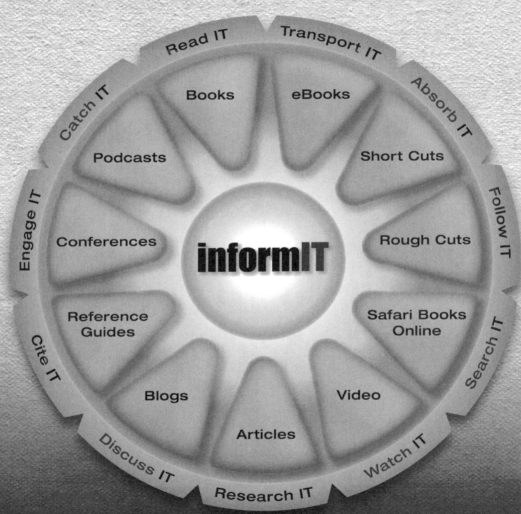

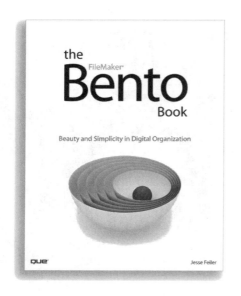

FREE Online Edition

Your purchase of **the Bento Book** includes access to a free online edition for 45 days through the Safari Books Online subscription service. Nearly every Que book is available online through Safari Books Online, along with more than 5,000 other technical books and videos from publishers such as Addison-Wesley Professional, Cisco Press, Exam Cram, IBM Press, O'Reilly, Prentice Hall, and Sams.

SAFARI BOOKS ONLINE allows you to search for a specific answer, cut and paste code, download chapters, and stay current with emerging technologies.

Activate your FREE Online Edition at www.informit.com/safarifree

> **STEP 1:** Enter the coupon code: XCDUHXA.

> **STEP 2:** New Safari users, complete the brief registration form.
> Safari subscribers, just log in.

If you have difficulty registering on Safari or accessing the online edition, please e-mail customer-service@safaribooksonline.com

     Adobe Press    Cisco Press   Press IBM Press   lynda.com Microsoft Press New Riders

O'REILLY Peachpit Press PRENTICE HALL que Redbooks SAMS SAS Publishing Sun   WILEY